THE BIBLE, **LIVE!**

THE BIBLE, LIVE!
EXPERIENCE-CENTERED ACTIVITIES FOR CHILDREN

Israel Galindo

Judson Press
Valley Forge

This book is for

Brandon

Cody

Douglas

Jacelyn

Jaimie

Kristen

Steven

Thomas

Contents

Introduction

WE'VE ALL HEARD THE AXIOMS: "CHILDREN LEARN BY DOING," "Experience is the best teacher," and "Don't tell—show!" While these axioms are universally accepted self-evident truths, the fact is we don't often practice what we preach. This book is a collection of interactive, experience-centered Bible learning activities for children, based on the idea that children indeed learn best by doing and that the most effective learning happens when they discover truths for themselves.

The educational approach used in *The Bible, Live!* puts the emphasis on active learning, as opposed to teacher performance. Instead of focusing on content, the book emphasizes learning through experience. Rather than relying on a teacher's expertise, activities exploit the natural learning potential of the learners. Rather than trying to motivate learners externally, lessons tap into children's natural desire to learn what is important to them at their own time and at their own pace.

Active Learning

The most effective teaching approach for children is active learning:
- active learning is an adventure
- active learning is fun and captivating
- active learning involves everyone
- active learning does not rely on teacher expertise
- active learning is achieved through participation
- active learning capitalizes on natural learning abilities
- active learning results from answering meaningful questions, explorations, reflection, interpretation, and application

Active learning is a nonschooling approach. The educational dynamics involved in these activities are discovery learning and two-way conversation between teacher and learner. As children participate in their learning experience, the teacher engages them in reflection and analysis by asking questions and involving them in conversation. In this way, the children are not merely entertained or kept busy by doing an activity. They learn to reflect and make connections between what they do and what they are learning about self, God, church, and faith.

Active learning is experience oriented. Children are concrete learners. Abstract concepts important to the life of faith—faith, trust, justification, salvation, hope, justice, law, right and wrong, mercy, grace, and so forth—are difficult if not impossible for them to grasp. Children need concrete ways to experience, see, touch, and feel these concepts in order to understand them. Only when they can experience these dynamics of faith will they become real for them.

Active learning is intergenerational. Children's faith is not formed in a vacuum; it is shaped through their being a real part of the life of their church. Therefore, it is important for children to get to know and feel loved and appreciated by as many adults and teens in the church as possible. These programs offer an element of intergenerational learning by providing a way for children to come in contact with program leaders from all age groups in the church. Children will get to know people they ordinarily would not come in contact with in the course of their regular church participation. Some of these programs can be led by youth. Others are ideal for grandparents and senior citizens in the church. Some programs can be led by people with disabilities, by young adults, and by couples in the church.

Active learning is intentionally educational. While the programs are creative and fun, they are not just entertainment. The intent is not to keep children busy but for the experience itself to teach a Bible truth. Some programs use common children's activities, like making a collage or working on a craft. It is the context in which the children participate—the church and the seasons, themes, and actions of the church; and the interchange between teachers and learners—that makes the Bible-to-life connection possible. Therefore, it is important that teachers not ignore suggested dialogue or questions for exploration in the teaching process.

Active learning is Bible based and Christ centered. The programs in this book are Bible based and Christ centered. They deal with themes in the all-encompassing life of faith from a biblical perspective. Each learning experience addresses issues and themes central to the lives of children with the intent of helping children appreciate the Spirit of Christ in their lives. Children will become familiar with the Bible as they read and respond to passages that reflect themes relevant to their lives.

Rules for Success

Experience teaches that the most successful learning happens when we follow certain basic rules. Failure to follow these rules may lead to a learning experience that is less than it could be for both children and leaders. Without becoming slaves to them, learn to trust these rules and follow them as best you can.

1. Never invite children into a vacuum. Children learn best when there is a healthy balance between structure and freedom to discover. Be intentional about the learning process from the minute children walk into the room by making it inviting, by having your materials organized, and by welcoming and directing the children to their places.

2. Keep it simple. Allow the children to stretch their imagination. Children have the capacity to take great pride in less-than-perfect products of their own making ("I made this!"). And they don't need to be pampered. Remember, the emphasis is on their learning and discovering Bible truths for their lives, not on teacher performance. While you will want to use the best materials available, simpler is almost always better.

Most of the learning activities in this book are suitable for children from grades two to six, and most can be completed in one hour. With a little modification, children in kindergarten and first grade can easily engage in these learning experiences. For younger learners, tell the Bible story rather than have the children read it, simplify the projects, and be more directive in engaging them in guided conversation. If you have a large group of children with mixed grades from kindergarten to sixth grade, encourage the older children to help the younger ones. That mentoring relationship in itself provides wonderful opportunities for mutual learning.

3. Tolerate chaos, but maintain discipline. Children will enjoy the learning experience best with the right mix of freedom and boundaries. Establishing rules early in the program and for each lesson will help children and leaders enjoy a more productive learning experience.

4. Final important rule: Have fun!

SECTION ONE

ADVENT

1. Advent Banner Workshop

This creative Bible learning experience will help children learn the meaning of the Advent season by leading them to identify the symbols associated with Advent and their meanings. Children will choose a favorite Advent symbol used in their church or home and will create a banner to use in their homes during the Advent season.

Materials Needed
- felt pieces (8½" x 11" for each child)
- glue or glue gun
- thin dowel rod (9" long for each child)
- symbol templates (optional)
- scissors
- string or yarn
- fabric paint (optional)

Preparation
Children will need room to spread out and work on their banners, so provide plenty of table surface. Children may also work on the floor, but provide covering to protect the floor surface or carpeting from glue.

For this learning experience, it is best that the church building be decorated for the Advent season. Tour your church sanctuary and buildings ahead of time to find symbols and decorations associated with the season of Advent: candles, liturgical colors, Advent wreaths, Advent banners. *(See Recommended Resources for books that depict and explain many symbols of Advent and Christmas.)*

Beginning the Learning Experience
1. As the children arrive, welcome them by name and lead them to have a seat in the room. Seating children as soon as they arrive will prevent the more restless ones from wandering around the room and getting into materials.
2. Dialogue with the children about the season of Advent. Ask about some of the things your church does during Advent. Encourage children to talk about some of the things they do at home to observe Advent.

Exploring
3. Let the children know that they will make banners to help them observe Advent. Lead them on a brief tour of your church buildings and sanctuary to find symbols of the Advent season. You can do this by playing "I Spy." Children are to wait till you say, "I spy a symbol of Advent that…" and describe a feature of the symbol. The children are to raise their hands and try to guess the symbol. [Example: "I spy a symbol of Advent that reminds us that Jesus is the Light of the world" (candle).]
4. Return to the classroom and distribute materials for the Advent banners. Instruct the children to choose an Advent symbol and an appropriate phrase (offer some suggestions based on your tour). They should draw the symbol on felt and cut out the shape to paste on the banner.

To insert dowel for hanging, just cut four slits near the top of the banner (see illustration). Then tie the string for hanging.

Concluding the Learning Experience
5. Conclude the experience by allowing the children to share their banners with the class. They should explain the Advent symbol and tell about the phrase they have chosen. End your time together in a prayer of thanksgiving for the season of anticipation.

2. Advent Symbols

Children are very receptive to the symbols of their faith. It does not take much prompting for them to learn the meaning behind the names and the symbols of the seasons of the Christian year. This Bible learning activity will help children identify, name, and describe the symbols of Advent in their church.

Materials Needed
- Bibles
- Advent Symbols Acrostic worksheet
- Advent Symbols filler pages
- markers and/or crayons
- three-ring binder (with slip front for cover)

Preparation
This activity will take place during the Advent season in the church after the church has been decorated with the symbols of the season. Before this learning activity familiarize yourself with your church's symbols and decorations by touring the sanctuary and buildings. Identify as many symbols and their meanings as you can: candles, Advent wreath, banners, colors, greens, Chrismons, evergreen trees, etc. Prepare the three-ring notebook by creating a colorful cover for it titled "Symbols of Advent in My Church" by the children of (name of church). This learning activity can be completed in one hour.

Beginning the Learning Experience
1. As the children arrive, greet them by name and invite them to work on the Advent Symbols Acrostic worksheet.
2. Give the children a few moments to work on identifying as many signs and symbols as they can; then review their answers. Help them identify any they may have missed.

Exploring
3. Announce that you will all go on a "symbol hunt" as a group through the church. Instruct the children that as you lead them around the church they are to point out symbols of Advent in the church. Make the sanctuary the highlight of your trip. Allow the children to find as many Advent symbols as they can in the worship room.
4. Return to the room and distribute the Advent Symbols filler pages, markers, and crayons. Tell the children that they will create an Advent symbols notebook for their church to help others learn about the symbols of Advent. Encourage the children to illustrate as many symbols as they remember from their "symbol hunt" and to write a brief description of the meaning of the symbol in the space provided. As the children complete the Advent symbols pages, have them punch holes on the sheets and place them in the binder.

Concluding the Learning Experience
5. When the children have completed the notebook, place it in an appropriate place for display such as the church foyer or a welcome center.

Advent Symbols Acrostic

Use the first letter of the words Advent, Season, and Christmas to name
as many symbols of the seasons of Advent and Christmas as you can think of.
Name as many as you can for each letter.

A _____

D _____

V _____

E _____

N _____

T _____

S _____

E _____

A _____

S _____

O _____

N _____

C _____

H _____

R _____

I _____

S _____

T _____

M _____

A _____

S _____

Advent Symbols Acrostic

Suggested Words

A angel

D donkey

V Virgin Mary

E evergreen tree/color, excelsis deo

N Nativity scene

T tallow candles, tree

S sheep

E earth (peace on earth), Emmanuel

A Advent wreath

S star

O organ music

N Noel

C carols, census, candles, camel

H holiday, halo

R red, reindeer

I Immanuel, incense, Immaculate Conception

S shepherds

T trimmings, town (of Bethlehem)

M Mary, manger, magi, myrrh

A adore

S songs, St. Nicholas

Advent Symbols in My Church

Name of symbol:

_____

_____

_____

_____

_____

_____

What this symbol means:

_____

_____

_____

_____

_____

_____

_____

3. Jesse Tree

The Jesse Tree is a tree (evergreen or other) decorated with symbols from the Old Testament and New Testament that depict the heritage of the Messiah, Jesus Christ. Based on Isaiah's prophecy that "a shoot shall come out from the stump of Jesse" (Isaiah 11:1), the Jesse Tree is a wonderful tool—a kind of theological family tree—that traces the stories of God's faithfulness in keeping the promise of providing a savior (or messiah) for all people. This learning experience will help children learn key Bible stories related to the promise of the Messiah and will provide them with a new Advent family tradition.

Materials Needed
- Bibles
- drawing paper, construction paper
- colored pencils, markers, crayons
- Jesse Tree Symbols handout
- scissors
- hole punch
- string
- flip chart or chalkboard
- glitter glue (optional)
- glue or glue sticks
- yarn of various colors
- lids and bottoms of frozen juice cans
- clear contact paper
- planted branch or small evergreen tree

Preparation
If you are able, make a sample Jesse Tree for the children to see. You can order a book of ready-to-cut color symbols for the Jesse Tree from Fortress Press: *The Jesse Tree*, by Raymond and Georgene Anderson, but you can easily make up your own set of Jesse Tree symbols. Make photocopies of the Jesse Tree handout for the children. This activity can range from one hour to two one-hour sessions, depending on how many symbols you allow the children to make.

Beginning the Learning Experience
1. Welcome the children as they enter the room. When they are settled and focused on you, challenge them to name as many kinds of trees as they can in one minute. Give one volunteer a stopwatch or watch with a second hand to keep time. He or she will call time when a minute is up. As the children call out names of trees, write them on the board.

2. Review the names of trees the children have called out, and point out that there is one tree you don't see up there: the Jesse Tree (in the unlikely event that someone has identified a Jesse Tree, use the opportunity to have that child explain what a Jesse Tree is).

Exploring
3. Distribute Bibles and have the children look up Isaiah 11:1. Explain that the Jesse Tree is a small tree decorated with symbols portraying the spiritual heritage of Jesus. "It is a kind of family tree that was suggested by Isaiah's prophecy: 'A shoot shall come out from the stump of Jesse'" (Isaiah 11:1). (Raymond and Georgene Anderson, *The Jesse Tree*, Philadelphia: Fortress Press, 1966, p. 4).

4. Tell the children they will make symbols for their own Jesse Tree. Distribute the Jesse Tree Symbols handout, Bibles, and art materials. After reading the corresponding Bible passage, the children will decorate their symbols.

OPTIONAL: You can paste the symbols on lids from frozen juice cans and decorate with glitter glue. Use a hole punch (or a nail if using the juice can tops) to make a hole for the yarn loop for hanging on the tree. If you wish, you can provide clear contact paper to paste over the symbols.

5. As the children work on their Jesse Tree symbols, ask exploratory questions about the symbols they work on: "Do you know what the story behind that symbol is?"

"Can you tell me what this symbol has to do with Jesus?" "Who can tell me the story of this symbol?"

Concluding the Learning Experience

6. Encourage the children to place their Jesse Tree symbols on the tree branch or evergreen tree you've provided. At home, children can add one symbol to the tree for each day of the week during Advent, or they can hang them all at once. End your time together in prayer thanking God for the promise of the Savior.

Jesse Tree Symbols*

Below is a list of recommended symbols and their Scripture references
for your Jesse Tree. If you do not want to make all the symbols,
you may make one for each week of the Advent season.
In that case, choose the symbol for the week that is most meaningful to you.
For each day during Advent, or each week, hang the symbol
on your Jesse Tree and read the Scripture verse.

	ADVENT TIME	SYMBOL	BIBLE VERSE
FIRST WEEK	Sunday	Jesse Tree symbol	1 Samuel 16:1-13
	Monday	The World	Genesis 1:24-28
	Tuesday	Adam & Eve	Genesis 3:1-24
	Wednesday	Noah & the Ark	Genesis 6:11-22; 8:6-12
	Thursday	Abraham	Genesis 12:1-7; 13:2-18
	Friday	Isaac & the Ram	Genesis 22:1-14
	Saturday	Jacob's Dream	Genesis 27:41–28:22
SECOND WEEK	Sunday	Rose of Prophecy	Isaiah 9:2-7; 35:1
	Monday	Joseph & His Coat	Genesis 37:1-36
	Tuesday	The Law	Exodus 20:1-17
	Wednesday	Aaron's Blessing	Numbers 6:22-27
	Thursday	Samuel & the Word	1 Samuel 3:1-21
	Friday	David	1 Samuel 16:14-23
	Saturday	Shepherds	Psalm 23
THIRD WEEK	Sunday	Solomon's Wisdom	1 Kings 3:3-28
	Monday	Elijah & the Ravens	1 Kings 17:1-16
	Tuesday	Elijah & Healing	2 Kings 5:1-27
	Wednesday	Isaiah the Prophet	Isaiah 6:1-8
	Thursday	Jeremiah the Prophet	Jeremiah 31:31-34
	Friday	Nehemiah the Builder	Nehemiah 1:1-4; 2:1-5; 7:1
	Saturday	Angels	Hebrews 1:1-14
FOURTH WEEK	Sunday	Zechariah & Elizabeth	Luke 1:5-25
	Monday	Mary	Luke 1:26-38
	Tuesday	Magnificat	Luke 1:39-56
	Wednesday	John the Baptist	Luke 1:57-80
	Thursday	Joseph	Matthew 1:18-25
	Friday	Bethlehem	Matthew 2:1-12
	Saturday	Birth of Jesus	Luke 2:1-20
	Christmas Day	Christ the Lord	John 1:1-18

*Adapted from Raymond and Georgene Anderson,
The Jesse Tree: Stories and Symbols of Advent. Philadelphia: Fortress Press, 1966.

SECTION TWO

CHRISTMAS

4. Christmas Story TV Box

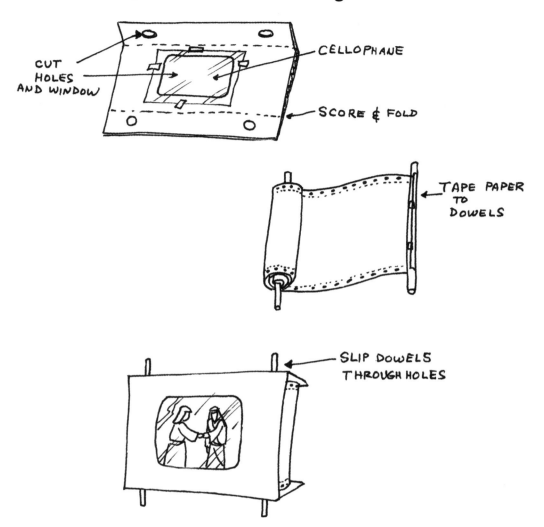

CUT HOLES AND WINDOW

CELLOPHANE

SCORE & FOLD

TAPE PAPER TO DOWELS

SLIP DOWELS THROUGH HOLES

Recounting familiar stories is an important community function. Repetition of stories learned by heart is one of the most powerful learning methods we have, and retelling stories in new ways promotes higher levels of learning: comprehension, evaluation, analysis, and synthesis. This learning experience will prompt children to review the familiar Christmas story and will allow them to retell it in their own ways.

Materials Needed
- Bibles
- computer fanfold paper
- dowels (at least two for each TV story box)
- cardboard boxes (at least 20" x 20" square) or cardboard panels 22" x 20"
- masking tape
- crayons, markers, pencils, pastels
- catalogues, magazines with Christmas themes photos and drawings (optional)
- scissors, X-acto knife
- cellophane wrap

Preparation

Depending on the time you have or on your safety concerns, you may want to cut out the "TV screen" on the cardboard boxes or panels ahead of time. The screen opening should be no larger than 7½" x 10" with rounded corners to simulate a TV screen. Use caution and supervision when allowing children to work with sharp cutting instruments. This activity can be completed in an hour.

Beginning the Learning Experience

1. Invite the children to sing Christmas carols and hymns that tell the story of the season, such as "While Shepherds Watched Their Flocks by Night" and "The First Noel."

Exploring

2. Share thoughts about how important it is to retell favorite stories. Retell the Christmas story by reading a children's storybook that faithfully follows the biblical events, or you may choose to show a tape of the Linus soliloquy of the passage in Luke from *It's a Charlie Brown Christmas.*

3. Distribute Bibles and invite the children to read along in their Bibles with the Christmas story found in Luke 2:1-20.

4. Distribute materials and instruct the children to create some scenes that retell the Christmas story in their own way (encourage them to work in teams). Using the computer paper (and being careful not to tear the perforations), they are to draw scenes in sequence. Children may choose to cut out Christmas pictures from magazines and catalogues to create a story montage. When they have completed their story sequence on the computer paper, they are to tape one dowel to each end of their story strip and roll it to make a scroll.

If you have not already done so, guide the children in constructing the TV "screen" by cutting out an opening (no larger than about 7½" x 10" with rounded corners to simulate a TV screen) in the cardboard box. Tape a tightly stretched sheet of cellophane on the inside of the opening. Cut openings for the dowels about 3" from the face of the screen opening on top and bottom.

OPTIONAL: You can also use cardboard panels (or poster board) instead of boxes. Score the top and bottom of the panel and fold back. Tape a tightly stretched sheet of cellophane on the inside of the opening and cut openings for the dowels about 3" from the face of the screen opening. Attach the story scroll to the TV by slipping the dowel ends through the holes. Children will turn the dowels to scroll from one side to the other to show their story scenes.

Concluding the Learning Experience

5. Conclude this learning experience by having the children retell the Christmas story using their TV story boxes.

5. Gingerbread Manger

 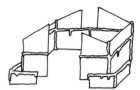 

Gingerbread houses are favorites during the Christmas season. This variation of an old holiday tradition will help children remember the true meaning of Christmas.

Materials Needed
- Bibles
- graham crackers
- animal crackers
- cake icing (ready to spread from cans and in squeeze tubes)
- plastic spoons and knives
- waxed paper
- cake sprinkles for decorating (optional)
- various types of candies for decorating
- recording of Christmas music (optional)
- cardboard sheets

Preparation
Make a sample "gingerbread manger," experimenting with ways to make construction easy. With newsprint, protect the table surface area on which the children will work. This activity can be completed in one hour.

Beginning the Learning Experience
1. Welcome the children as they arrive and have them take a piece of cardboard and tear a sheet of waxed paper to work on, then have them be seated to wait for your instructions.
2. Distribute Bibles and have children read Luke 2:1-7. Invite the children to recount the story of Mary and Joseph's trip to Bethlehem and of the birth of Jesus in the manger.

Exploring
3. Tell the children that they will be making a "gingerbread manger" to remind them of the story of Jesus' birth in Bethlehem. Show the gingerbread model you made and demonstrate how you constructed it. Children are to use panels of graham crackers for the walls and roof of the manger, cake icing as "glue" and for decorations, animal crackers for the animals in the inn (no elephants!), and various types of candy for decorations. They can shape a manger from small panels of graham crackers. Be sure the children build their mangers on the cardboard covered with waxed paper so they can take the craft home with them.
4. As children work on their gingerbread manger project, play Christmas music in the background (optional) and ask exploratory questions like: "Do you remember why Mary and Joseph went to Bethlehem?" "Do you think it was a comfortable trip?" "Do you think they were nervous?" "How do you think they felt when they could not find a room to sleep in?" "What do you think Mary was thinking/feeling when it came time for the baby Jesus to be born?" "How did God take care of Mary, Joseph, and Jesus during this time?"

Concluding the Learning Experience
5. Continue to ask exploratory questions as the children work. When the children are done with their projects, ask them to help you by cleaning up after themselves. Pause to pray together giving thanks to God for providing for Jesus and his parents and for providing for us today.

6. Voices in the Manger

This learning experience will encourage children to explore the gift of the Incarnation by creating characters and engaging in a guided dramatic dialogue.

Materials Needed
- Bibles
- large sheets of construction paper
- scissors
- craft foam
- string, yarn
- glue or glue sticks
- box for a "manger"
- crèche

Preparation
This learning experience will exercise children's imagination. A manger setting for the guided dialogue will help children engage in the experience more readily. Provide a cardboard box with straw and a blanket for a manger (or if you have a manger, use it). Use a doll wrapped in "swaddling cloths" for the Christ Child. Make the manger set as elaborate as you desire. This learning activity can be done in one hour.

Beginning the Learning Experience
1. Greet the children by name as they enter and invite them to visit the crèche on display for a few minutes. Engage the children in conversation about the crèche, its characters, the animals depicted, its style, its use. Ask them to share about a crèche they may have at home or about where they have seen one.

Exploring
2. Distribute Bibles and invite the children to read the story of the birth of the Christ Child in Luke 2:1-19. With the children, explore the story by asking questions related to how Joseph and Mary arrived at

the inn and how they wound up at the manger. Ask questions about how they felt and what they may have been thinking. Ask similar questions about the shepherds.

3. Direct the children to choose a character or animal they identify with in the story or in the crèche. Instruct them to make a mask depicting the character (Mary, Joseph, angel, shepherds) or animal (donkey, sheep, cow, and so forth), using the materials you've provided: construction paper, craft foam, yarn, glue, string, and so on. Be sure they cut out openings to allow them to see through their masks.

4. When the children are finished making their masks, gather them into the manger area and lead them in a dramatic dialogue. As children get into character, guide them to speak from behind their masks as you take them through the story of the birth of Jesus. Your dialogue questions may go something like this:

✱ Joseph and Mary have just arrived at the manger. Joseph, what are you thinking?

✱ Mary, what are you feeling being so far away from home?

✱ Mary, are you nervous about the baby being born in this place? Why?

✱ Cow, what are you thinking as you watch these strangers move into your manger?

✱ Donkey, what are you thinking as Joseph takes some of your straw to place in the manger?

✱ Sheep, what do you say to the other animals about what is going on this strange night?

✱ Joseph, what do you wonder as you see the light of the bright star in the sky above?

✱ Shepherds, how are you feeling as the angels appear? What do you wonder about?

✱ Cow, what do you make of all the noise the little human child is making as he is born?

✱ Joseph, how do you feel when you see that the baby is born safe and healthy?

✱ Mary, how are you feeling holding the baby Jesus in your arms?

✱ Donkey, what do you wish you could tell the mother and father of the baby?

Continue your guided dialogue developing the story as you go. Take some cues from the children's responses for follow-up questions and exploration of what it may have felt like to witness the scene.

Concluding the Learning Experience
5. End your time together by singing "Away in a Manger." Close in a prayer thanking God for the gift of the Christ Child.

7. Nativity Mosaic

The Nativity marks the turning point in God's relationship with us as it points to the Incarnation event—Emmanuel ("God with us"). This Bible-learning experience will help children think about this endearing symbol of God's love for us.

Materials Needed
• Bibles
• Nativity template handout
• confetti or multicolored paper
• glue, paper plates, and cotton swabs
• pictures and prints of the Nativity
• 3" x 5" cards with the letters of Emmanuel printed one letter to a card

Preparation
You will need copies of the Nativity template handouts for each child; you may copy the template onto light-colored construction paper if your copy machine can handle that kind of paper. Purchase confetti in a craft store, or just cut up different colored tissue and construction paper into small (no larger than 1/2") shapes. Use paper plates to hold the glue and cotton swabs for applying the glue. This learning activity can be completed in one hour.

Beginning the Learning Experience
1. Begin this Bible learning experience by leading the children in singing some Christmas carols and hymns that mention the manger: "Away in a Manger," "O Little Town of Bethlehem," "While Shepherds Watched Their Flocks by Night," or other favorites.
2. Distribute the set of 3" x 5" cards on which you have printed the letters of the name Emmanuel one letter to a card. Shuffle the cards and spread them on the table, challenging the children to unscramble the word. Once they've figured out the word, talk to the children about what it means: "God with us."

Exploring
3. Distribute Bibles and lead the children to read Luke 2:1-17. Talk with the children about the story of Jesus' birth in a manger. Review with them why Jesus was not born at home. Ask about what the shepherds heard and saw. Discuss how this event represents how God relates to us in a new way through the Incarnation. Ask a volunteer to read Isaiah 7:14 and refer back to the name Emmanuel they unscrambled. Explain how this was a promise from God, given long before Jesus' birth.
4. Show various prints and pictures of Nativity scenes from books, magazines, and posters. Direct the children to identify the characters and to describe things they see in the scene. Ask exploratory questions about how the artist chose to depict the scene. Point out the artist's use of colors and composition.
5. Distribute copies of the Nativity template handout, confetti, glue, and cotton swabs. Encourage the children to be creative as they create their own Nativity scene by pasting the colored confetti onto their Nativity scene in a mosaic style.

Concluding the Learning Experience
6. Conclude your learning experience by having the children display their work and by singing "Away in a Manger."

The Nativity

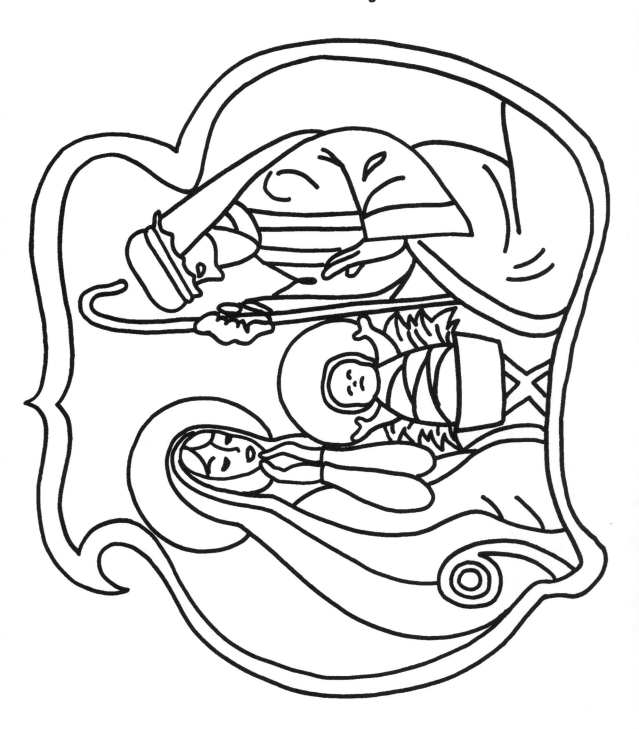

SECTION THREE

LENT

8. Foot-Washing Frieze

This messy active learning experience will challenge the children with an opportunity for artistic expression and will help them learn about Jesus' object lesson in humility. Advise parents to plan in advance so children may be dressed appropriately (especially girls, who might wear tights).

Materials Needed
- Bibles
- large strips of butcher paper for frieze (3' x 6'). Optional: If you want each child to take a painting home, you can set down a large piece of construction paper for each one in the painting area on the butcher paper.
- pencils or crayons
- tempera, finger paint, or washable paint (purple, blue, red, white, and yellow)
- newspapers
- baby wipes
- towels
- basin of soapy water
- masking tape
- paper plates or shallow containers for paint

Preparation
Set up a part of the room for the painting activity. Tape the large painting frieze surface to the floor with masking tape. Place newspaper on the surrounding floor to protect it from paint. Set washbasins, towels, and wipes in a nearby corner.

Beginning the Learning Experience
1. When the children enter, greet each by name and ask each to have a seat at the table or in chairs placed in a circle. When they are focused on you, remind them of the Lenten season that the church is observing. Tell them that today they will learn about one of the most important moments in the lives of the Jesus and his disciples.

Exploring
2. Distribute Bibles to the children and have them look up John 13:1-10,12-17. (Write this reference on the board so the children can copy it later.) You can have the children read this in parts: narrator, Jesus, Peter. Or tell the story in dramatic fashion, or read it out of a contemporary version.

When you've read the story, ask exploratory questions: "Why did people wash feet in those days?" [Because the roads were dusty, and it was a sign of hospitality to wash the feet of a guest.] "Is this something we do today?" [No.] "Why or why not?" [Most people wear shoes to protect their feet, and our sidewalks aren't dusty.] "What did Peter say to Jesus when he was about to wash his feet?" [Peter asked Jesus not to wash his feet.] "How do you think Peter was feeling at that moment?" [Embarrassed. Confused.] "Why do you think Jesus insisted that Peter let him wash his feet?" [Jesus wanted to show his disciples how to treat one another. He wanted them to be humble and not think they were better than others.] "Have you ever washed someone else's feet?" "What did Jesus teach his disciples by washing their feet?" [He wanted to teach them to serve one another in love.]

3. Tell the children they will, as a class, make a large Footprint Frieze(s) to remember this Lenten story. Instruct the children to remove their shoes and socks. [Note: if a child does not want to participate in the painting, he or she can help a teacher with the footwashing.]

OPTIONAL: The children can make individual footwashing posters by laying down single sheets of construction paper.

Inform the children about the proper procedure for this activity. In order for the painting to be colorful, the colors should not be mixed into each other too much. You can use pencil or crayon to "block" designs on the frieze or the papers. Lead the children, about two at a time, to step into the paint palette and "paint" on the frieze with their feet. Each child should use only one or two colors at most. Children can paint abstract forms or try to paint designs using toes and heels.

Concluding the Learning Experience
4. Once the children have finished painting, they are to go to the washbasin area where a teacher or another student will wash their feet with the soapy water and/or baby wipes. As you wash the children's feet, say something like, "Jesus washed his disciples' feet as a way of teaching them that they are to serve one another. Remember Jesus' lesson." Ask the children to be good servants by helping to clean up the room after the activity.

9. Lenten Gift Poster

Lent is a good time to teach about giving and self-denial. During this penitential season, Christians are encouraged to practice spiritual disciplines to help them grow in faith. This learning activity will help children practice giving in a thoughtful and disciplined manner.

Materials Needed
- Bibles
- Poster board for each child
- crayons
- markers
- Lenten/Easter theme stickers
- small envelopes (6 for each child)
- Bible verse stickers
- pennies
- glue
- sparkle glue (optional)
- deck of cards (preferably children's playing cards with numbers on them)
- a bag or hat from which to draw the cards (optional, a number spinner or numbered dice)
- sponge shapes for stamping
- shallow dishes for paint
- purple and yellow tempera paint
- paper towels
- prepare poster with the heading "My Lenten Gifts"
- paper plates

Preparation
Prepare surface areas to protect them from paint. Make a sample Lenten gift poster. Encourage the children to be creative when making their own posters. Children will need a lot of space to work on their projects. You may be able to use easels or tack the poster boards onto the wall; be sure to protect the wall from paint also. This learning activity will take about an hour.

Beginning the Learning Experience
1. Welcome the children as they enter the room, and invite them to sit at the table. When they are focused, ask, "Who can tell me what season we're in?" [Lent.] Tell them that we want to learn about ways to observe and celebrate this season in which we remember how Jesus sacrificed (gave) his life for us.

Exploring
2. Tell the children that you are going to play a game called "More and Less." The object of the game is to have the least number of cards by the end of the third round.
3. Remove the face cards from the deck of cards, and place the remaining cards in a hat (or comparable container). The teacher picks a card out of the hat and reads the number.

The teacher asks the first child, "More or less?" The child answers "More," if she thinks she will draw a card with a higher number, and "Less," if she will try to draw a card with a lower number.

If the child guesses right, she gives up the card. If she guesses wrong, she must hold on to the card, which will count against her. That child shows her card to the next child and asks him, "More or less?" The game continues until all children have had a turn. Continue for three rounds to see who has the least number of cards.
4. Have a volunteer read the story of the widow's offering in Mark 12:41-44 (or you may read the story from a children's story book). Ask exploratory questions about the story: "Did the widow give more or less than the others?" "How can less be more?" "What do you think Jesus meant when he said she gave more?"
5. Say, "During Lent we take time to think about the gifts we offer to God and the spirit in which we give them." Tell the children that

they will make a Lenten Gift Poster to help them remember to give to God in the right spirit during this season.

6. Show a sample of the Lenten Gift Poster. Encourage the children to be creative when making their own. Distribute poster board to each child and a set of six small envelopes. Children are to label each envelope with a day of the week, except Sunday. They will paste the envelopes on the poster to create pockets. Using the purple and yellow paint and the stamp sponges (or other objects), they are to decorate the poster. Allow them to paste the poster title, "My Lenten Gifts," to the poster when they are finished.

Concluding the Learning Experience

7. As the children leave, give each two pennies to put in the envelope that corresponds to, or which is closest to, the day of the week on which they are doing the activity. Encourage them to continue to place their Lenten gifts in the envelopes so they can bring an offering to church as the widow did.

10. Lenten Symbols

Children can appreciate the symbols of their faith, often in ways that adults cannot. It does not take much prompting for them to learn the meaning behind the names and the symbols of the seasons of the Christian year. This Bible learning activity will help children identify, name, and describe the symbols of Lent in their church. *(See Recommended Resources for books that depict and explain many symbols of Lent and Easter.)*

Materials Needed
- Bibles
- Lenten Symbols in My Church "filler pages"
- Signs and Symbols handout
- markers and/or crayons
- three-ring binder (with slip front for cover)

Preparation
This activity will take place during the Lenten season in the church after the church has been decorated with the symbols of the season. Before this learning activity, familiarize yourself with your church's symbols and decorations by touring the sanctuary and buildings. Identify as many symbols and their meanings as you can: candles, Lent banners, liturgical colors, crosses, posters, etc. This learning activity can be completed in an hour.

Beginning the Learning Experience
1. As the children arrive, greet them by name and invite them to work on the Signs and Symbols handout.

2. Give the children a few moments to work on identifying as many signs and symbols as they can, then review their answers. Help them identify any they may have missed.

Exploring
3. Announce that you will all go as a group on a "symbol hunt" through the church. Instruct the children that as you lead them around the church, they are to point out symbols of Lent in the church. Lead the children around the church buildings to point out the symbols of Lent your church uses. Make the sanctuary the highlight of your trip. Allow the children to find as many Lenten symbols as they can in the worship room.

4. Return to the room and distribute the Lenten Symbols filler pages, markers, and crayons. Tell the children that they will create a Lenten symbols notebook for their church to help others learn about the symbols of Lent. Encourage the children to illustrate as many symbols as they remember from their "symbol hunt," and to write a brief description of the meaning of the symbol in the space provided. As the children complete the Lenten symbols pages, have them punch holes on the sheets and place them in the binder.

Concluding the Learning Experience
5. When the children have completed the notebook, place it in an appropriate place for display such as the church foyer or a welcome center.

Lenten Symbols in My Church

Name of symbol:

_____

_____

_____

_____

_____

_____

What this symbol means:

_____

_____

_____

_____

_____

_____

_____

_____

Signs and Symbols

1.

2.

3.

4.

5.

6.

7.

8.

9.

10.

11.

12.

13.

14.

11. Nails of Love

The crucifixion of Jesus is central to the Passion story and to the story of our personal faith. Often adults shy away from dealing with this violent episode in the life of Christ when teaching children. But children have great capacity to understand and appreciate this expression of love at their own level. They can trust "Jesus died for me," as an expression of God's love for them in a way that is authentic for their faith. This creative Bible learning experience will help them remember that Jesus died for them.

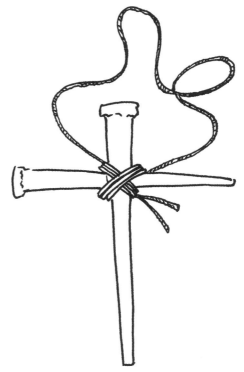

Materials Needed
• Bibles
• wire
• wire cutters
• masonry nails
• string
• glue gun (optional)
• background music (optional)

Preparation
Cover any surface areas on which children will be working to protect them from glue. For younger children you may want to use heavy string instead of wire. This will help prevent them from sticking their fingers with the sharp ends of the wire. This learning activity will take forty-five minutes to an hour to complete.

Beginning the Learning Experience
1. When the children have settled down and are focused on you, remind them that this is the season of Lent. Explore with the children the focus of this season of the church year: the death of Jesus on our behalf, leading to the Resurrection, which we will celebrate on Easter Sunday.
2. Explain that the story of Jesus' crucifixion is a source of both sadness and joy for us. Ask them to think about why this might be so [because Jesus suffered and died, and because he died to save us because he loves us].

Exploring
3. Distribute Bibles and invite the children to read part of the story of Jesus' crucifixion and about something that happened afterward. Direct the children to read John 19:16-19, and then John 20:24-28.
4. Explore the Bible story with the children by asking exploratory questions: "Who is this story about?" "Who else is this story about?" [It is also about us.] "Where did the soldiers take Jesus?" [To prison.] "Why did they take him there?" [Because they wanted to crucify him; because some men accused him.] "Why do you think this happened to Jesus?" [Because some people did not believe in him; because he had to die for us.] "Do you think this is a sad story? Why?" "We say that Jesus died for us. What do you

think that means?" "Why did Thomas not believe that Jesus was alive again after his crucifixion?" [Because he did not see him with his own eyes.] "What did he say he needed to see in order to believe?" [To see with his own eyes.] "Did he believe in the end? How do you know?" [Yes, because he said, "My Lord and my God."]

5. Tell the children that they will make a Lenten cross of nails to help them remember Jesus' death on the cross during this Lenten season and to remind them that Jesus died for them. Distribute two masonry nails to each child, two lengths of wire (each about 4"), and string (about 15-20") for hanging their crosses around their necks.

6. Show the children how to make a cross with the nails and how to wrap the wire to bind the nails together; use a simple crosswise wrap. (Optional: placing a drop of glue from the glue gun will make this easier for the children. Have them blow on the glue to help it dry before they wrap the wire around the nails.) To complete the cross, attach a piece of string to the nail at the top of the cross of nails (see illustration).

Concluding the Learning Experience

7. When all the children have completed their crosses of nails, encourage them to reflect on the meaning of the symbol by asking, "When you wear your cross, what will it remind you of?" [That Jesus died for me and rose from the grave.] End your session in prayer, thanking God for the love shown through Jesus on the cross.

12. The Women

Women played an important part in Jesus' life and work. During the time of Jesus' greatest need, women figured prominently. This Bible learning activity will highlight the role of women disciples and provide a way for children to deal with grief.

Materials Needed
- Bibles
- boxes for making memory boxes (see description below), one for each child
- paints and brushes
- rags and cleaning materials
- glue
- buttons (optional)
- dry macaroni and noodles (optional)
- glitter (optional)
- stickers (optional)
- volunteer actors to play the roles of the women

Preparation
Cover all surface areas to protect them from paint and glue. For smaller children, be sure to use smocks to protect their clothing as well. Secure volunteers to deliver the monologues for step three. Encourage the volunteers to study the Scripture passage and create female biblical characters who would have been eyewitnesses to the accounts related in the Scripture text. Have the actors prepare a monologue based on their reading and interpretation of the biblical text.

Beginning the Learning Experience
1. As the children arrive, welcome them and seat them at the worktable. Remind them that this is the season of Lent. For the sake of new learners in the room, explain that Lent is a time of preparation and reflection on the death of Jesus, leading to his resurrection. Ask children to share about what they know about the season of Lent and about Jesus' Passion (his final week) and crucifixion.

2. As dramatically as you can, set the stage of the street scene that Jesus encountered on the day of his crucifixion: rough streets, a hot day, a curious and jeering crowd, mean soldiers, and so forth. Have a volunteer read the account of the women in the crowd found in Luke 23:27-31. Explain that these women loved Jesus and were very sad. Ask the children questions about how people in the crowd felt: some angry, some confused, some sad.

Exploring
3. Introduce the volunteer actors who will perform a monologue. Have each actor dressed in costume and stay in character throughout her time with the children. Ask each to give emphasis to her character's feelings and to the questions of how and why Jesus, a good person whom people loved, was treated in such a way.

4. Explore with the children how the women must have felt seeing Jesus, a good man and the Son of God, being treated this way. Ask them how they feel when something bad happens to people they love. Ask them to share examples of when that happened to them. Acknowledge that this is one of the hardest questions we deal with in all our lives.

5. Explain that even though sad things happen to us, God is always with us and will send people to help us, as God sent Simon and the women to help Jesus. Tell the children that they will make a "memory box" to remember this lesson. Explain that a memory box is a special box to use during scary or sad times. In it are things that will be reminders of how God and others have helped them in the past. It helps them remember that God is with them even when they feel afraid or sad.

6. Guide the children in the construction of memory boxes. There are many ways to make memory boxes. Get different shaped papier-mâché boxes from craft stores, get pre-cut wooden pieces to glue together for wooden boxes, or use simple pencil boxes. These can be decorated with buttons, dry macaroni and noodles, stickers, paint, markers, stain, and glitter.

Concluding the Learning Experience

7. When the children complete their memory boxes, they are to put one or two things in them that reminds them (a) of a sad or scary time and (b) of how God and others helped them through that time. They can draw a picture, write a note, hunt for an object that reminds them of the above, cut a picture out of a magazine, etc.

OPTIONAL: provide objects for children to put in their boxes: a Scripture verse, a stone, a slip of the paper with "God is always with me" written on it.

8. Conclude your Bible learning experience with a prayer expressing thanksgiving for God's faithfulness in being with us in sad and scary times.

SECTION FOUR

EASTER

13. Bible Easter Eggs

JESUS ROSE!

Decorating Easter eggs is a favorite project with children. This learning experience will allow children to focus on the meaning of Easter while enjoying a favorite activity.

Materials Needed
- Bibles
- food coloring or store-bought egg kit
- hard-boiled eggs
- string, buttons, pieces of felt
- glue or glue gun
- wax crayons
- colored markers (permanent)
- Easter theme stickers (optional)

Preparation
You may want to prepare ahead of time for this activity by asking the children to bring their own hard-boiled eggs. Have some extra eggs handy for any who may have forgotten to bring some. Prepare sample Bible Easter Eggs ahead of time to show the children. This learning activity can last from thirty minutes to a full hour.

Beginning the Learning Experience
1. When the children are settled, distribute Bibles and invite them to share in a reading of the Easter story in Mark 16:1-14. Review the story with the children by asking content and exploratory questions: How many women went to the tomb? Can you tell me their names? When did they go to the tomb? Why did they go to the tomb? What were they worried about concerning the tomb? What did they find when they got there? Who did they meet there? What did the young man tell them? How did the women feel when they heard the news? When Mary Magdalene told the others that Jesus was alive, did they believe her? Did Jesus appear to anyone else other than the women? Jesus seemed upset with them. Why?

Exploring
2. Lead the children to make Bible Easter Eggs of the characters in the Bible story they've just studied. They may choose instead to decorate their eggs with symbols relating to Easter. Distribute eggs and follow directions from any egg decorating packet sold in stores or use food coloring for dying the eggs.
3. While the eggs are drying, help children decide which Bible characters they will create to remind them of the Easter story. Distribute materials for decorations.
4. As the children work on their Bible Easter Egg characters, ask them about why they chose that character or symbol and about what role that person played in the story or what the symbol means. Children may work on as many eggs as time allows.

Concluding the Learning Experience
5. As children complete their Bible Easter Egg characters, encourage them to retell the Easter story using their egg characters. Encourage them to share their stories with their families.

14. Easter Baskets, Bonnets, and Hats

Easter is the joyful celebration of life in the triumphant, risen Christ. This learning experience will help children express that joy by creating colorful baskets, bonnets, and hats in preparation for an Easter parade in which they will celebrate the risen Savior.

Materials Needed
- Bibles
- feathers and plumes
- plastic fruit, eggs, and knick-knacks
- glue guns
- string or wire
- plastic flowers
- straw baskets, bonnets, hats
- ribbon and felt pieces
- scissors

Preparation
Children will need lots of room for this activity, so provide enough space to allow them to spread out. Cover work surface areas to protect them from glue. Inexpensive straw hats and baskets can be purchased at craft stores, or you may instruct the children to bring their own. (Have one or two on hand for those who may not bring a hat or basket.)

Beginning the Learning Experience
1. Begin this learning experience by playing a game of Hangman with the word Easter. When the children have guessed the word, ask them to tell you about what Easter means and why we celebrate that day.

On a chalkboard or large piece of paper, draw six short lines across the top of the page, one blank for each letter of the word Easter. Ask the children to guess letters.

Each correct guess (i.e., an A, E, R, S, or T) should be filled in the appropriate blank(s). For each wrong guess (i.e., any letter not appearing in the word), draw a single line that will eventually represent a gallows and hanged stick figure. In other words, low on the paper or board, start with a horizontal line; then above it, draw a perpendicular vertical line; then add another horizontal line, this one at a right angle meeting the top of the vertical line and stretching to its right. Then, at the right end of the second horizontal line, add a short vertical line going down approximately one-fifth to one-eighth the length of the parallel vertical line. (This is your gallows.) Then, at the end of that short line, draw a circle representing the head of the hanged person. As the game progresses and wrong guesses continue, add a vertical line for the torso and then angled lines for the arms and legs. (If necessary, you may even go to the extent of adding eyes, nose, mouth, fingers, toes, etc.)

2. Distribute Bibles and lead the children to read John 20:1-18.

Exploring
3. Spend a few minutes exploring the Bible passage with the children. You may want to have children play the characters in the story and act out the passage as you narrate the story again. Ask exploratory questions to contrast the sadness the disciples must

have felt after Jesus' crucifixion with the joy those same disciples experienced after they learned about his resurrection.

4. Announce to the children that the class will go on an Easter parade to express joy for Jesus' resurrection. Tell them that in order to join in, they must create some expressions of joy by making Easter baskets, hats, and bonnets. Invite the children to create their parade attire using the materials you've provided. Encourage them to be as outlandish as they can with their creations, gluing and wiring flowers, ribbons, plastic fruit, ornaments and knick-knacks, plastic eggs, etc., to their baskets and hats or bonnets.

Concluding the Learning Experience

5. When the children have completed their creations, lead them in an Easter parade. To express the joy of the resurrection event, they will shout, "Jesus is risen!" and "Hosanna!" as they parade and encounter bystanders.

15. Jesus Lives!

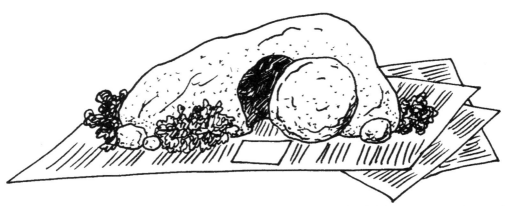

Jesus' resurrection is the cornerstone of the Christian faith. By making an empty-tomb sculpture, children will create a symbol of Jesus' resurrection to use in sharing the good news that Jesus lives!

Materials Needed
- Bibles
- self-drying clay or cornstarch dough (see recipe below)
- black and white tempera paint
- paper plates
- stiff 2" paint brushes
- newspapers
- paper towels or wipes
- Spanish moss

Preparation
Make cornstarch dough in advance. Mix two cups of cornstarch and four teaspoons of baking soda with about 2 1/2 cups of cold water. Cook over medium heat and stir for about five minutes until mixture thickens. Allow dough to cool, add one-half cup of white glue (such as Elmer's) and knead for about five minutes. This recipe makes enough dough for two sculptures.

Store the dough in an airtight container. When exposed to air, the dough will dry hard and can be painted. Experiment with the dough and make a model of the empty tomb sculpture for the children to see as they make their own sculptures.

Mix one plate of gray paint by mixing some of the black and white tempera paint. Provide paper plates with black and white tempera colors also. You will want to cover working surfaces with newspapers for the children to work on. Younger children should wear smocks to protect their clothing from paint spatters.

Beginning the Learning Experience
1. Begin this Bible learning experience by asking the children what special day will be observed in this season. [Easter.] Invite them to share what they like best about Easter. Ask them to explain what Easter is all about. [Jesus' resurrection.] Ask them what makes Easter Sunday so special. [It is the day we celebrate that Jesus lives.]

Exploring
2. Distribute Bibles and invite the children to read together the Bible account of Jesus' resurrection in Luke 24:1-10.
3. Share with the children that you can think of a symbol of Jesus' death. Allow them to guess the symbol of the cross. Talk about what the symbol represents: Jesus' sacrifice for us. Ponder with the children what might be some good symbols for Jesus' resurrection.

Allow them to suggest several and to talk about why they think they are appropriate symbols (e.g., butterfly, cocoon, egg, lilies, etc.). Share with them that they will make a symbol for Jesus' resurrection they can use to share the good news that Jesus lives: an empty tomb, like the one the women encountered in the story.

4. Show your sample of the empty-tomb sculpture and suggest ways to make it. Distribute materials and allow children to create their sculptures by molding a hand-sized piece of dough into a "tomb" and then carving out a "cave" in the center. Using the material they carved out of the center for the cave, instruct them to shape the stone (in the shape of a disk or wheel) that covered the tomb and place it in front of the tomb opening but to the side. They may sculpt smaller "stones" to decorate their sculpture as they wish.

5. To finish the empty tomb sculpture, they can dip the stiff brushes in the black, white, and gray tempera paint and splatter their sculptures to give them a pebbled look. Allow the sculpture to dry.

Concluding the Learning Experience

6. Distribute the wipes and encourage the children to clean their hands. To conclude the lesson, gather the children around their sculptures as they wait for them to dry. Lead them in a guided conversation by talking about their sculptures and what they symbolize. Ask them to think about what they will share with others when they show their sculptures. Ask them about where they want to display their models. Lead them to think about how the empty tomb is an appropriate symbol for Easter. End your time together in prayer thanking God that Jesus lives today.

SECTION FIVE

BIBLE

16. Bible Diorama

Children are familiar with many Bible stories, and they may have some they consider favorites. This learning experience gives children the opportunity to interpret a favorite Bible story by translating it to three-dimensional space. By creating a diorama, a miniature three-dimensional scene depicting Bible characters in a story, children will choose how best to depict the message of the story.

Materials Needed
- Bibles
- poster board with diagram for box construction (or shoe boxes)
- markers and crayons (or watercolor paints)
- scissors
- glue or glue gun
- pipe cleaners
- Play-Doh
- masking tape
- string
- miscellaneous materials and knick-knacks for diorama props
- construction paper
- cellophane wrap

Preparation
Prepare a model diorama. Provide children's Bible picture books or coloring books with Bible themes to help children gain ideas for their dioramas. This project will take about an hour to complete.

Beginning the Learning Experience
1. Welcome the children as they enter the room by calling them by name and directing them to be seated at the worktable.
2. Explain that the Bible is a book of wonderful stories. Share some of the Bible story picture books, and ask the children to think silently about their favorite Bible story for a minute because you will ask them to share it with you and the class.

Exploring
3. Allow some time for each of the children to share a favorite Bible story. Engage them in dialogue by asking probing and interpretive questions: "Who is the story about?" "Why do you like the story?" "What does it teach us about God and ourselves?" "How did the people in the story feel about what was happening to them? Has anything

like that happened to you?" "Does the story have a happy ending?" Help each child identify the chief characters in each story, and ask about the setting of the story.

4. After each child has had a chance to share a story, tell the class that today they will make a way to share their favorite Bible stories with others. Show the children the sample diorama you have made and share the story it depicts. Explain the characters and the background of your diorama and how you made it.

5. Offer the children the opportunity to work in groups, in pairs, or individually. Distribute the poster board for their box construction (or shoe boxes if you will provide them). Give instructions about painting or drawing a background and about how to construct the box. (Younger children will need help with this.)

To construct a box out of poster board, score the sheet into a nine section grid. (It will look like a large tic-tac-toe game board.) Cut out the four corner sections of the grid. You will have one center section with four flaps in the shape of a cross. Cut one inch off the edge of the outer four flaps. Fold the flaps along the score marks to form the box, and then tape it together.

The background can be painted or drawn, or children can choose to cut out construction paper shapes (mountains, sun, clouds, windows, furniture, doors, etc.). When children complete the background, they may start on the figures and props for their dioramas.

Demonstrate how to make figures out of pipe cleaners. Encourage the children to be creative about how they want to make their figures. Dialogue with them about their choices of materials and about how best to interpret the Bible story in their dioramas.

6. As children work on their project, ask exploratory questions: "What scene are you making?" "What are the people in your scene doing?" "Why do you think this is a good story?" "What do you think people will learn when they see your diorama?" "What did Jesus teach about this situation?" "How do you think your character felt when this event happened?"

Concluding the Learning Experience

7. After the children complete the background and have placed their figures in the diorama box, cover the front with a film of cellophane and attach it to the box with masking tape.

8. Have the children put their dioramas in a display area. As you have time, have each child share the Bible story the diorama depicts and what the story teaches.

17. Bible Story Scavenger Hunt

There are many ways to learn and review a Bible story. This learning activity will prompt children to learn, identify, and match central elements of some favorite Bible stories. You can adapt the procedure for use with any Bible story you are trying to teach your learners.

Materials Needed
- Bibles
- 3" x 5" cards for Bible reference cards
- Bible story objects (described below in Exploring)
- miscellaneous items for the "Which Does Not Belong?" activity

Preparation
Ahead of time, gather the Bible story objects as described below. Distribute and hide them in a designated area for the scavenger hunt. You may adapt the suggestions to best fit your needs by choosing different Bible stories or by adding more items for the scavenger hunt. This activity will take about an hour.

Beginning the Learning Experience
1. Begin this active learning experience by playing "Which Does Not Belong?" Gather any number of items you may have handy and group them according to some predetermined category: things you use in school, things you use in church, edible things, old things, things you write with, things you wear, and so forth. For each set of items, include one thing that does not belong. For added suspense, keep things hidden (under a towel or behind a panel) until you are ready to let the children see the objects. Instruct the children to look carefully at the items set before them and, when they think they know what object doesn't belong in the category, to raise their hands and whisper to you which one does not belong and why. Continue to play until you are ready to move on to the next step. Tell the children that this fun activity was practice for their next activity: a Bible story scavenger hunt!

Exploring
2. Distribute Bibles and divide the children into two smaller groups; have no more than four children in each group. (For more small groups, plan for an additional Bible story and set of scavenger hunt items.) Give each group a 3" x 5" card with the Bible reference for their story and direct them to read it together. Make one reference card for the good Samaritan (Luke 10:30-37) and one card for Moses and the burning bush (Exodus 3:1-8).

3. When the groups have finished reading their assigned passages, instruct them in the Bible story scavenger hunt. Each team is to search the designated areas for articles associated with their Bible story. They must collect all five items related to their story and return them to home base. As children return an item to home base, ask them to explain their rationale for connecting the item to their story. Team members must not return with an item from another team's Bible story; if they do, the team member who returns it must observe a "time out" (about three minutes) before entering the hunt again. The first team to collect all of its items wins.

SAMPLE ITEMS:
FOR THE GOOD SAMARITAN
- money purse with coins
- donkey (photo, picture, or toy)
- Band-Aid or first-aid kit
- photo or brochure of hotel or motel
- map of Samaria

FOR MOSES AND
THE BURNING BUSH

• burnt matches
• angel figurine or picture
• branch (for bush)
• sandals
• empty container of milk or
  jar of honey

Concluding the Learning Experience

4. When each team has collected all items corresponding to their Bible story, have them review the story by explaining how each item relates to their Bible story. Ask exploratory questions about their assigned story to encourage comprehension. "Who is the main character in this story?" "What happened to that person?" "Why did that happen to him or her?" "Has something like that happened to you?" "Did God respond in the story? In what way?" "What do you think the story teaches us?" "What other items would you include in a scavenger hunt for this story?"

18. The Bible Lamp

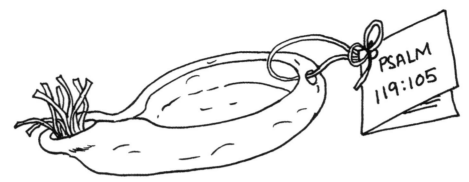

PSALM 119:105

Learning to value the Bible as a guide to faith and living is necessary for leading the Christian life. This Bible learning activity will help children learn about the importance of the Bible and will help them remember that the Bible is to be a lamp for their feet and a light for their path.

Materials Needed
- Bibles
- self-drying modeling clay
- flashlight
- candle with candle holder
- matches
- black tempera paint
- newspaper for covering work surface
- tinsel (optional)
- yarn
- rags or paper towels
- paper plates for the paint
- 3" x 5" cards
- glue
- markers
- hole punch

Preparation
Prepare a sample of the Bible lamp. Some Bible dictionaries and encyclopedias have pictures of ancient Palestinian oil lamps the children can use to model their lamps. Use the candle in a candle holder to prevent accidents. This learning activity will take about an hour.

Beginning the Learning Experience
1. Challenge the children to name as many sources of light as they can in one minute. As the children call out their answers, write them on the board. Discuss with the children the many ways light is used and the ways that having light helps us.

Exploring
2. Have the children look up Psalm 119:97-105 in their Bibles. (Avoid using The Living Bible for this lesson; it is a poor paraphrase of the original.) Children can take turns reading a verse until the passage is read. Then go around the room and ask each child in turn to share one thing he or she understands about the passage. Encourage students to interpret the passage. Ask: "What do you think that means?" "Can you give me an example?" "How does the writer feel about the Word of God?"
3. Focus on Psalm 119:105. Ask the children to share how they think the Word of God (the Bible) can be a light for our feet. Invite the children to help you with an object lesson. Give one child the flashlight, and one child the candle in a candle holder. Explain that the term "lamp" in the passage refers to an oil lamp people used to light their homes in ancient times (show the sample lamp you've made). Show how understanding that background can teach us a lesson about faith. Ask the children

with the candle and flashlight to stand against a wall across the room. Light the candle and turn off the lights in the room. Ask the child with the flashlight to turn it on and walk across the room. Point out to the children that the beam of light shines all the way across the room, so the child can walk confidently across to the other side. Instruct that child to demonstrate and then to turn off the flashlight.

Demonstrate how the child holding the candle illustrates the meaning of the passage, "your word is a lamp unto my feet," by pointing out that the light from the candle (lamp) gives only enough light to take one step at a time. Point out that this is an illustration of our faith: often, God gives us enough faith (light) to take one step at a time without knowing what lies farther ahead. Trusting God means taking one step in faith at a time. The Bible teaches us how to have this kind of faith. Ask the child to demonstrate taking one step at a time into the light by walking across the room holding the candle before him or her.

4. Distribute material for making the Bible Lamp. Cover the work surface with newspaper and direct the children to shape a Bible Lamp as referred to in the Bible passage. Once they have shaped their lamps, dab black tempera paint around the wick area to simulate smoke stains.

OPTIONAL: glue small streamers of tinsel to simulate flame/light.

Instruct the children to punch a hole on the back of the lamp large enough to loop a piece of yarn.

Concluding the Learning Experience

5. Distribute a 3" x 5" card to each child. Fold the card in half. On the cover children are to write Psalm 119:105, and on the inside they are to write the verse: "Your word is a lamp to my feet and a light to my path." With the hole punch, punch a hole in the top left corner and loop the yarn through it. Attach the yarn to the lamp. Recite the verse as a group.

19. Bible Puppet Workshop

This learning experience will help children translate their knowledge of a Bible story into creative dramatic play.

Materials Needed
- Bibles
- socks for puppets
- glue guns
- Tacky Glue
- newspaper for table cover
- scissors
- "google eyes"
- buttons
- felt and felt pieces
- cloth pieces
- yarn
- cardboard
- cotton balls
- photos or drawings of sample hand puppets

Preparation
Allow the children plenty of space to work on their projects. Keeping materials on a separate table from work areas and keeping the work areas clean will help with discipline. Use caution when using glue guns around children. This learning activity takes about an hour to complete.

Beginning the Learning Experience
1. Welcome the children as they enter the room. Direct them to sit at the table. (Try to have photos or drawings of puppets on the table for them to look at while they wait for the lesson to start.) Having quiet music playing in the background helps set a good mood for the experience. Turn off the music when you are ready to begin the lesson.

2. Choose one of the following Bible stories to work on. The children will create their puppets based (loosely) on the characters in the story. Later they may put on a play of the story using their puppets: the prodigal son (Luke 15:11-32), Jesus as a child at the temple (Luke 2:42-52), the good Samaritan (Luke 10:30-37). Have the children turn to the story in their Bibles and read it; they can take turns or read "parts."

Exploring
3. Explore the Bible story by asking open-ended questions such as, "What were some of the things you liked about your story?" "Why do you think this story is in the Bible?" "If you had to change your story for your puppet show, how would you change it and why?" "Do you think these stories really happened? How do you know?" Help them explore both the meaning of the story and the characters involved. Ask: "What do you think this story teaches us?"

4. Explain to the children that they will put on a puppet play based on the story they've studied. Ask them to make a list of the characters they will need to appear in the play. Don't forget miscellaneous support cast as "crowds." If there are not enough characters in the story for the number of children, they can make up some. List the characters on the board with their characteristics. Ask: "What do you think this character was like?" "What do you think he or she should look like?"

5. Have children choose which puppet characters they want to make. Allow them to use their imaginations in creating the puppets—characters can be people or animals or made-up creatures.

6. Direct the children to get the materials they need to create their character puppets from the supply table (a sock, felt pieces, eyes, buttons, etc.). To make certain this happens in an orderly fashion, you may want to allow a small group to go at a time. Distribute glue, scissors, and so forth, as

needed. Teachers can help with the glue gun.
7. As children create their puppets, you can play soft music in the background and ask them questions about their characters and the story. This is an important learning step; do not skip it. As the children work, ask exploratory questions: "How do you think your character felt when this event happened?" "How do you think your character will sound?" "What do you think your character should look like?" "What do you think about the way your character reacted in the story?"

Concluding the Learning Experience

8. Provide a broom and a wastebasket, and have the children help with the cleanup. If time allows, conclude this learning experience by encouraging the children to perform a puppet play based on the Bible story they have selected.

20. Interview a Bible Character

Dramatic interpretation of biblical characters brings the Bible alive for children. This learning experience will help children understand that stories about persons in the Bible are about real people, just like them.

Materials Needed
• Bibles
• volunteers in Bible character costume
• Interview Questions handout (or create your own)
• microphone and camcorder or tape recorder (optional)
• reporter's outfit (e.g., trench coat, hat, notepad)
• My Favorite Bible Character worksheet

Preparation
There are any number of ways to do a Bible-character interview. If you have a volunteer who can do good impromptu characterizations, then children can choose to interview their favorite or familiar Bible persons. Otherwise, planning a more scripted interview may be more appropriate. Remember that what will make this type of learning experience a success is imagination—allowing your children to believe that the person before them is really a Bible character. Even older children can get into the mood and play along if properly invited. In preparation for this learning experience, provide a list of questions for your Interview Questions handout and prompt your volunteer as to the interview questions you will ask. Help the volunteer learn more about that Bible character by reading about him or her in a Bible dictionary, commentary, or Bible encyclopedia. Have your actor dress in costume and remain in character throughout the learning experience.

Outlined below is just one way to lead this Bible learning experience. Vary it as your needs and resources warrant. This learning activity takes about one hour to complete.

Beginning the Learning Experience
1. As the children enter the room, welcome them and have them begin to fill out the My Favorite Bible Character worksheet.
2. Ask children to share their responses to the worksheet. If the Bible character you are prepared to present is on a child's handout, tell that child, "You're in luck because you'll get to meet you favorite Bible character today." (If no one chooses the character you've prepared, tell the children you want to present a favorite Bible character of yours.)

Exploring
3. Conduct the interview. Dress one or two of the children in a "reporter's outfit."
OPTIONAL: Other children can play sound crew with a tape recorder or video crew with a camcorder.

Give your reporters the Interview Questions for your Bible character. Your reporters are to ask the Bible character these questions, but encourage them and the rest of the children to ask other questions they may have. Introduce your Bible character to the children as he or she enters the room and has a seat. Let the interview begin.
4. When the interview is over, invite the children to learn more about the Bible character by looking up Bible stories and references concerning the Bible character.

Concluding the Learning Experience
5. Close your session in prayer by thanking God for the men and women of the Bible who teach us more about God and Jesus.

Interview Questions

Interview Questions for Peter

1. Can you tell us your name please?
2. Do you have a nickname? What is it?
3. Where is your hometown? Where were you born?
4. What do you do for a living?
5. What made you famous enough to get your name into the Bible?
6. Did you know Jesus?
7. How did you meet him?
8. What was it like to be with Jesus?
9. What is your favorite memory of being with Jesus?
10. What do you think is the most important lesson you learned from Jesus?
11. Some people say you denied Christ. Can you tell us about that?

Interview Questions for Martha

1. Are you the Martha in the Bible?
2. Where did you live?
3. What are some things you enjoy doing?
4. Do you have any brothers and sisters?
5. Did you ever get upset with your brothers or sisters?
6. How did you meet Jesus?
7. What was he like?
8. What is your favorite memory of Jesus?
9. How did you become a follower of Jesus?
10. What is the most important lesson you learned from Jesus?

My Favorite Bible Character

1. Write the name of a favorite Bible character.

_____

_____

_____

2. Is the story of this person found in the Old Testament or New Testament? Do you know where?

_____

_____

_____

_____

3. What do you like best about this Bible character?

_____

_____

_____

_____

_____

4. If you could ask this Bible character one question, what would it be?

_____

_____

_____

_____

21. The Disciples

This learning experience will help children memorize the names of Jesus' twelve disciples and will encourage them to identify themselves as disciples of Jesus.

Materials Needed
- Bibles
- The Disciples handout
- Disciples Information Cards
- card stock
- pencils or markers
- stickers of your choice (stars, circles, rainbows, etc.)
- blank label stickers

Preparation
Make enough copies of The Disciples handout for every child. Copy the Disciples Information Cards (or glue them) onto card stock and cut apart. Hide the Disciples Information Cards throughout the room.

Beginning the Learning Experience
1. Welcome the children by name as they arrive. Begin by asking the children to define what a disciple is. See how many of Jesus' twelve disciples they can name. Encourage them to find the names of the disciples by looking in their Bibles in Matthew 10:2-4. Have the children share as much as they remember about each disciple.

2. Continue this learning experience by teaching the children the names of the twelve disciples. Using the following poem will make it easy to memorize the names. A good way to lead the group to memorize the rhyme is to write it on the board, have them repeat the poem, and then erase a word or two before repeating it again. Using different voices as you repeat the poem makes it even more interesting: yelling it, whispering it, using a "Mickey Mouse" voice, a "Goofy" voice, a "Barney" voice, a monster voice, a normal voice, and so forth. By the time you've erased all the poem, they should have it memorized.

THE TWELVE DISCIPLES
Peter, Andrew, James and John,
Fishermen of Capernaum,
Thomas and St. Matthew too,
Philip and Bartholomew,
James, his brother Thaddaeus,
Simon and the one named Judas,
Twelve disciples here in all,
Following the Master's call. [1]

Exploring
3. Distribute The Disciples handout. Instruct the children to work in pairs to find the Disciples Information Cards (be sure to remind them to leave the cards in place for other children to discover). First they are to memorize the facts about each disciple, as found on the card; then they must find and read to you the Bible reference about that disciple. When they have done so, they can write the disciple's name on the handout. They will continue for all the disciples in this manner. As children share two facts and read the Bible verse, give them a sticker to place beside the disciple's name.

Concluding the Learning Experience
4. When children have collected stickers for all the disciples, encourage them to recite the poem they learned earlier before earning their last sticker. To complete the collection of disciples, give children blank label stickers and have each write his or her own name on the label as a disciple of Jesus.

---

[1] *"The Twelve Disciples," is from Pamela Conn Beall and Susan Hagan Nipp,* Wee Sing Bible Songs *(Los Angeles: Price Stern Sloan, Inc., 1986). Used with permission.*

The Disciples

Disciples Information Cards

JAMES
DISCIPLE FACTS:
- Pastor of the church in Jerusalem
- Son of Zebedee
- Brother of John the disciple
- Bible Verses to Look Up:
  Matthew 4:21; 17:1

THADDAEUS
DISCIPLE FACTS:
- Little is known of him
- May have been called
  Judas, son or brother of James
- Bible Verses to Look Up:
  Luke 6:16; Mark 3:19;
  John 14:24

MATTHEW
DISCIPLE FACTS:
- Also called Levi
- Was a tax collector
- Wrote a book in the Bible named
  after him
- Bible Verses to Look Up:
  Luke 5:27-28

SIMON
DISCIPLE FACTS:
- A Zealot
- The disciple we know least about
- Bible Verse to Look Up:
  Luke 6:15

THOMAS
DISCIPLE FACTS:
- Did not believe Jesus was alive
  until he saw the wounds
- Also called "Didymus"
  meaning "twin."
- Bible Verses to Look Up:
  John 20:24-29

JUDAS
DISCIPLE FACTS:
- Kept the money purse for
  the disciples
- Betrayed Jesus for thirty pieces
  of silver
- Bible Verses to Look Up:
  John 12:4-6

Disciples Information Cards

PETER
DISCIPLE FACTS:
- Leader of the disciples
- Wrote two letters in the Bible
- Denied three times that he knew Jesus
- Bible Verses to Look Up: John 18:25-27

BARTHOLOMEW
DISCIPLE FACTS:
- He is also called Nathanael in the Bible
- Said, "Can any good thing come out of Nazareth?"
- Bible Verses to Look Up: John 1:45-46

ANDREW
DISCIPLE FACTS:
- Fisherman
- Peter's brother
- Brought some Greek people to Jesus
- Bible Verse to Look Up: John 1:40

JOHN
DISCIPLE FACTS:
- Fisherman
- Son of Zebedee
- Brother of James
- Wrote two books and three letters in the Bible
- Bible Verses to Look Up: Matthew 4:18-22; Mark 1:19-20

PHILIP
DISCIPLE FACTS:
- Fisherman
- Said, "Come and see."
- Jesus asked him where to buy food for 5,000 people
- Bible Verses to Look Up: John 1:43-46

JAMES
DISCIPLE FACTS:
- Son of Alphaeus
- Perhaps "James the Younger"
- Bible Verses to Look Up: Matthew 10:3; Mark 3:18; 15:40

SECTION SIX

CHURCH AND WORLD

22. Build a Church

This learning activity will help older children understand some of the elements involved in being and acting as the church. This activity can be as complex or as simple as you want to make it. You will want to tailor the material to fit your own church's profile, mission, and personality.

Materials Needed
- Bibles
- pencils, markers
- butcher paper or drawing paper
- one set of Build-a-Church cards per group
- copies of your church's newsletter

Preparation
Prepare enough copies of the Build-a-Church cards (see samples) for each group of children; three to five children per group works well. It may prove helpful to prepare for each group a "kit" that contains all the materials they will need for this activity. Become familiar with your denominational and church structures so you can provide appropriate guidance as the children design their churches. See the Facts section of the Build-a-Church cards for examples of specific characteristics and features. Substitute facts about your church for those on the sample cards. This activity, which is geared toward older elementary grade children, will take about ninety minutes.

Beginning the Learning Experience
1. Welcome the children as they arrive. Greeting them by name and asking them to be seated at the table will help the children remain focused from the start of the activity.
2. Ask the children how many of them are church members. Ask them to tell the story of how they came to be church members. (For most of them, it will be related to a baptism decision.) Explain that as members, as they grow older, they will be asked to help make important decisions about their church.

Explain that in order to do so, they will need to have a good understanding of how a church works. Tell them that to help them understand how a church works, they will build their own church.

Exploring
3. Explain the Build a Church activity to the class and give them a time limit to complete the learning activity.
4. Divide the class into smaller groups of between three to five children. You may want to instruct each group to assign themselves a Timekeeper and a Church Inspector to help things move along.
5. Distribute a set of Build-a-Church cards and writing materials (e.g., paper, pens or pencils) to each group. As the children do their work, be a resource by moving around to the groups and by offering suggestions, answering questions, and providing information. Do not hesitate to point out problems or inconsistencies in their reasoning and decisions, but stress that we all learn by our mistakes and by asking questions.

Concluding the Learning Experience
6. Call the groups back at the assigned time to have plenty of time for debriefing. Have them complete the Church Inspector's Inventory card as a final step.
7. Ask the children for the insights they have gained from this experience. Use questions like, "What did you learn about your church during this experience?" "What was the most difficult thing to decide?" "What do you understand are the main purposes of the church?" "Why do you think we do all the things we do at our church?" "What things did you design in your church that are different from the way we do church?"
8. Allow the children to share some of their questions about church. Share your own ideas about your church. Explore some ways the children can be involved in the life of their church.

Build-a-Church Cards

Card 1   Instructions

With the other members of your group, you must build a church from your understanding of what it means to be a (fill in your denomination) church. The only rules you must follow are:
• You must finish your church in the time allowed;
• You cannot vote on anything;
• You must use all the Build-a-Church cards;
• When time is called, your group must complete the Church Inspector's Inventory card.

Card 2   Membership

The decision to be a disciple of Jesus and to join his church is an important one. Long ago, many people were persecuted for joining the church. Today, many people around the world suffer because they choose to be disciples of Jesus.

   Deciding to become a member of the church is a wonderful but serious matter. As you think about your church, what will you tell people who want to join your church?
• Who will be allowed to join your church?
• Will anyone not be allowed to join?
• How old will people have to be to become members of the church?
• What will it mean when someone becomes a member? What will be different for that person?
• What three things will you expect of every member?

HINT: The following verses in the Bible may help you decide about church membership: Matthew 18:20; Acts 2:37-47; 13:1-5; Ephesians 4:11-12; Colossians 3:16-17

FACTS: [Teacher, include here some facts about your church membership, such as "Our church accepts people as members by (1) letter of membership from another church; (2) baptism; (3) statement of faith in Jesus Christ."]

Card 3   Missions

Missions is what the church does to express God's love in meeting the needs of the world. Answer the following questions about missions for your church:
• What kind of missions activities will your church do?
• Who will do missions?
• Will your church support local (in-your-neighborhood) missions?
• Will your church support missions in other countries?
• In what ways will your church support missions?

HINT: When you see someone, or a group of people, in need, there is a place for missions! Often, people in the church do missions when they feel a special call from God to do a unique work.

FACTS: [Teacher, include here some facts about your church and missions, such as what percentage of your church budget is given to missions, the names of missionaries your church has sent out, or how many groups your church supports with missions money or through direct participation.]

Card 4   Worship

Worship is one way we confess that God is God and that we are God's people. Decide how your church will choose to express worship to God. Answering the following questions may help you decide:
• Who will lead the worship experiences?
• How does your choice of a building affect worship?
• What kind of music will you have?
• What kinds of musical instruments will you have?
• Will there be a sermon?
• Will the Bible be read?
• Will the service be formal or informal?
• Will the service be somber or lively?
• Will there be a part for the children?
• Will there be prayer during the service?
• What special rituals will you observe?
• Will there be an opportunity for people to make an offering to God?
• What else will be different about the way your church worships?

HINT: What you believe about who God is and about what the church is will help determine your style of worship.

FACTS: [Teacher, include here a fact about your church's worship like, "We follow the Christian Year," or, "We celebrate worship in the Baptist (or Methodist or Lutheran or Episcopal, etc.) tradition."]

Card 5   Building Design

The building you choose for your church will determine many things. Use the following questions to help you think through what you need before you "start building," and then draw a diagram of your church building on the drawing paper.

- What shape will your worship room be? Why?
- How will you furnish the worship room?
- How many buildings will you need?
- Will you need classrooms? How many?
- What about parking space?
- What about access by handicapped persons?
- How many bathrooms will you need?
- What about location? (on a main street? in a residential neighborhood?)
- What will the outside of your building look like?

HINT: What do you want people to think when they see your church building? Will the building allow you to do all you want?

FACTS: [Teacher, include here some facts about your church building, such as how many buildings you have, when they were built, what style architecture they reflect.]

Card 6   Christian Education

Learning more about God, Jesus, the church, and yourself is important. Helping people grow strong in their faith is part of what Jesus told the church to do. Answer the following questions to help your group make decisions about education in your church:
- How will you help people learn about God in your church?
- How will you go about "making disciples" in your church?
- How will you help people grow stronger in their faith?
- Will you have classes for adults? What will they be like?
- Will you have classes for teenagers? What will they be like?
- Will you have classes for children and infants? What will they be like?
- Who will do the teaching?
- How many teachers will you need?
- What will be the five most important things you will teach in your church?

HINT: What you believe about God, Jesus, the church, and the Bible will help determine what you teach and how you teach it.

FACTS: [Teacher, include here some facts about your church's education program, such as "Our Sunday school has classes for all ages with forty teachers and four directors. There are twenty classes and about two hundred people come to study every week. We also have a preschool center for smaller children."]

Card 7   Music

It has been said that music is the language of the heart of God. Music is very important to the life of most churches: in worship, in missions, in education. Make decisions about music in your church by answering the following questions:
• What kind of music will you have for your church?
• Will you have musical instruments?
• Will you have choirs?
• Will you have performers and performances?
• When will music be heard in your church?
• Will you teach music in your church? Why or why not?
• Who will lead music in your church?

HINT: Your style of worship may determine what kind of music you choose.

FACTS: [Teacher, include here some facts about music in your church, such as "Our church has music programs for people of all ages, with three staff people responsible for music: choirs, handbells, organ, piano, plays, music for worship, and lots more."]

Card 8   Staff

Staff persons are people your church hires to help make the church work. Decide the following about your church staff:
• How many staff members does your church need?
• What staff positions will you need? (See list of possibilities below.)
• How much will you pay the staff members?
• Will your staff include both men and women?
• What will you call the staff positions? (See below for hints.)

CHURCH STAFF POSSIBILITIES

Pastor	Senior pastor	Youth minister/pastor
Education minister/pastor	Music staff	Children's minister/pastor
Missions staff	Office staff	Building staff
Assistant pastor	Church school director	

HINT: Decide what your church needs before hiring staff. Decide what each staff member does so that two people aren't doing the same thing.

FACTS: [Teacher, include here some facts about your church staff, such as how many people your church employs and their titles, how long they've been at your church, how many senior pastors your church has had, etc.]

Card 9   Programs and Activities

Decide what kind of activities your church will offer. The cost for each activity you choose is shown below. Add the cost of the activity to your Budget Worksheet (Card 12).

Music program for children ($300)   Music program for preschool ($200)
Choir ($500)   Church bus ($20,000)
Sunday school ($3,000)   Youth program ($500)
Local mission program ($1,000)   Training for teachers ($300)
Senior adult program ($400)   Bible study ($500)
Wednesday night program ($1,000)   Wednesday night dinners ($3,000)
Counseling services ($500)   Church newsletter ($150)

HINT: You can make up any other program you want for your church. For every program, you will need a person to lead it and money to run it. Your programs should meet the needs of your church members and community.

FACTS: Our church offers many programs and activities. Read the church newsletter to see all that goes on at our church!

Card 10   Stewardship and Budget

Every decision, activity, and program in your church will require money and resources of time, energy, materials, and/or talents. For every decision you make about your church, enter the resources or the amount of money you think you will need to make it happen.

Remember that you depend on your church members to provide the resources you will need to make ministry happen.

HINT: Base your budget on what you want to accomplish as a church. Your budget will be limited to how much money your church members are able or willing to give.

FACTS: Our total church budget this year is: $_____

Card 11   Location

Decide where you will locate your church. The cost of buying land is noted below. Enter the amount in your Budget Worksheet (Card 12).

Inner city   ($100,000)   Suburbs   ($250,000)
Small town   ($150,000)   In the country ($50,000)

HINT: Where you put your church building may determine what kind of things you will be able to do and what kinds of people will come to your church.

FACTS: Our church is located in the _____.

Card 12   Budget Worksheet

Item	Amount
1. Location	$
2. Staff members	$
3. Activities of the church	$
4. Gifts to missions	$
TOTAL	$
`How much will your members need to give?	$

Card 13   Church Inspector's Inventory

Make sure you have completed each major element in your Build-a-Church kit by checking off this inventory. When you have checked off all items (in any order), you have completed the task.

❏ Instructions   ❏ Membership   ❏ Missions   ❏ Worship

❏ Building Design   ❏ Christian Education ❏ Music   ❏ Staff

❏ Location   ❏ Budget Worksheet   ❏ Programs and Activities

❏ Stewardship and Budget

When you have checked off all items, prepare to share your plans for a church with the rest of the group.

Signature of Inspector

23. Church Year Poster

The Christian Year provides children with a way to appreciate the depth and breadth of their faith. This learning activity will help children learn and review the seasons of the Christian Year and associate significant personal life events with the church year emphases.

Materials Needed
- Bibles
- 11" x 14" paper
- markers, pencils, watercolor paints, and paint brushes
- blank mailing labels or blank colored self-stick labels
- Church Year Poster template
- various holidays theme stickers (optional)
- Holiday Matching Cards
- calendars with marked or referenced holidays

Preparation
Prepare a set of Holiday Matching Cards. Write the months of the year, one month on each 3" x 5" card. On other cards, write the names of familiar holidays and special events in your church, such as New Year's Day, Groundhog Day, St. Patrick's Day, Independence Day, Halloween, Christmas, and your church anniversary. Then copy the Church Year Poster template onto 11" x 14" paper, one for each child. This learning activity will take about an hour to complete.

Beginning the Learning Experience
1. Begin this learning experience by forming two teams of children. Distribute the Holiday Matching Cards. Team 1 gets the months cards, and Team 2 gets the holidays and special days cards. Challenge the teams to match the holidays with the corresponding months. When a child on Team 1 is given a holiday card by a member of Team 2, she should determine whether that the holiday belongs to her month card. (Refer to the calendar as needed.) If the holiday does not belong to her month, she should return that holiday card to the other child and he should try again with another child, on Team 1. Encourage the children to work together to match their holiday cards with the month cards as quickly as they can. If children are unsure of how to match a holiday to a month, work together as a class to complete the activity.

Exploring
2. Distribute Bibles and read together the following passages: Ecclesiastes 3:1-8 and 2 Timothy 4:2. Explore with the children the meaning of these passages.

3. Show the Church Year Poster and review the diagram highlighting the seasons of the church year and the months associated with them. Converse with the children about the emphases of each season: "How do you celebrate this season?" "What colors are associated with that season?" "What special things do you do to observe this season?" "What does that season cause us to think about?" "Which is your favorite season? Why?" "What best memory do you have for that season?" "Who do you think about during this season?"

Ask the children to write their names on the self-stick labels and place them on their birthday months on the poster. Ask them to name some holidays, write them on labels, and place them in the corresponding months on the poster. Encourage the children to think of other things to note on the poster (spring, winter, vacations, etc.).

4. Distribute copies of the Church Year Poster, markers, holiday theme stickers (optional), and invite the children to make their own posters. Instruct them to identify their birthdays and those of their family members. Family anniversaries, vacations, and other special events may be added. Encourage them to decorate their posters using the liturgical colors of the church year and to be creative with other decorative details.

Concluding the Learning Experience

5. Conclude the learning experience by having the children show off and compare their posters. Read again the passage in Ecclesiastes, and end your time in prayer thanking God for the gift of time and seasons.

The Church Year

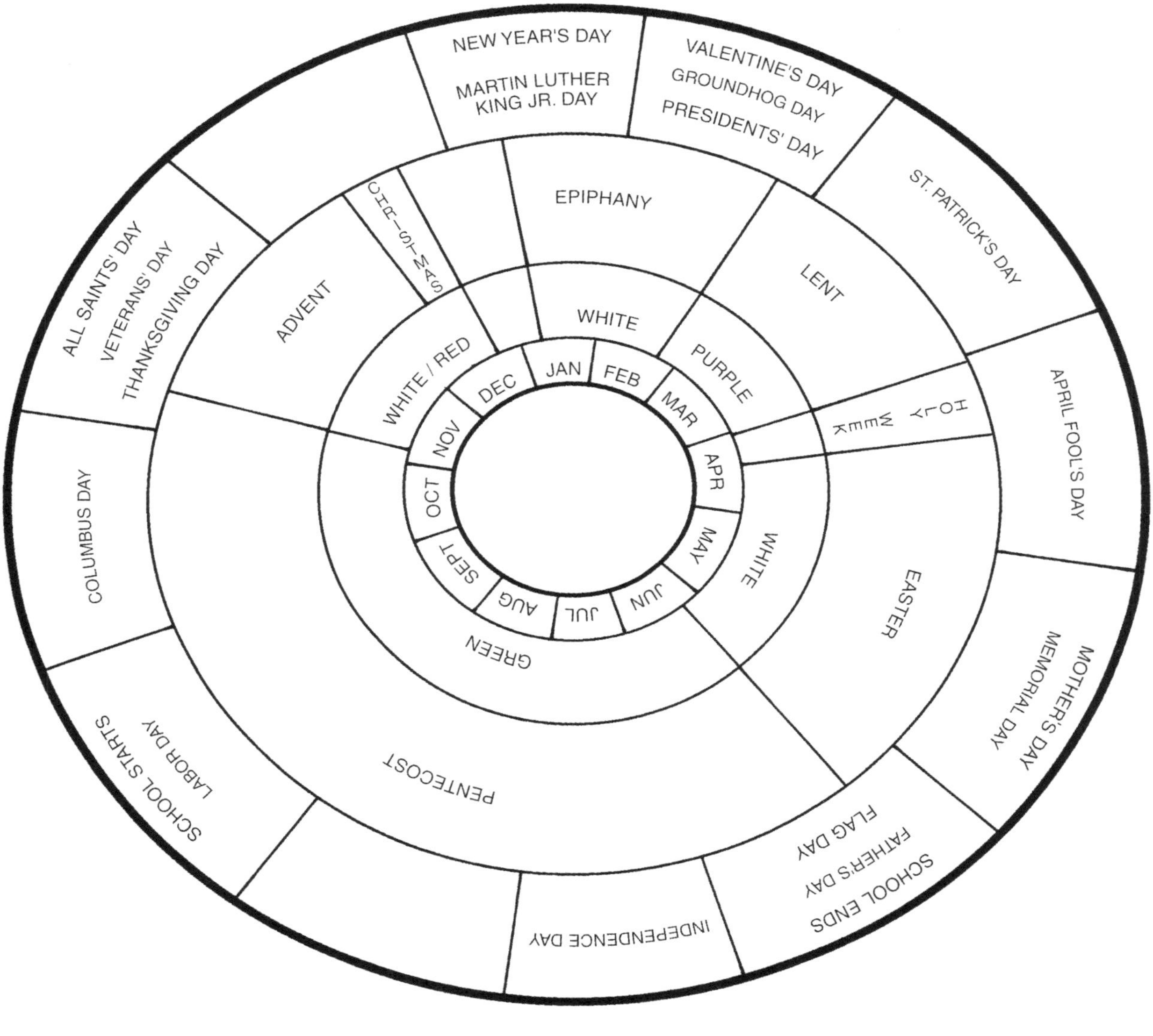
NEW YEAR'S DAY
MARTIN LUTHER KING JR. DAY
VALENTINE'S DAY
GROUNDHOG DAY
PRESIDENTS' DAY
ST. PATRICK'S DAY
APRIL FOOL'S DAY
MOTHER'S DAY
MEMORIAL DAY
FLAG DAY
FATHER'S DAY
SCHOOL ENDS
INDEPENDENCE DAY
SCHOOL STARTS
LABOR DAY
COLUMBUS DAY
ALL SAINTS' DAY
VETERANS' DAY
THANKSGIVING DAY
ADVENT
CHR-IST-MAS
EPIPHANY
LENT
HOLY WEEK
EASTER
PENTECOST
WHITE / RED
WHITE
PURPLE
WHITE
GREEN
JAN
FEB
MAR
APR
MAY
JUN
JUL
AUG
SEPT
OCT
NOV
DEC

"There is a time for everything, and a season for every activity under heaven."

—Ecclesiastes 3:1

The Church Year

"There is a time for everything, and a season for every activity under heaven."

—Ecclesiastes 3:1

24. Design a Worship Service

Welcoming children to participate in worship by teaching them how to do so is one of the most important things a church can do for its children. This Bible learning experience will help children learn about how their church worships by guiding them to intelligently design a worship service for Children's Sunday or Children's Sabbath.

Materials Needed
- Bibles
- chalkboard or flip chart
- pencils and paper
- felt-tipped pens
- thick black markers
- Children's Sunday Text worksheet (for bulletin divisions)
- Children's Sunday Picture worksheet (for bulletin cover)
- hymnals
- samples of the worship bulletin of your church
- dictionary

Preparation
Work with your church's worship planning group or the church staff to make this a memorable learning event for the children. Plan ahead to find ways of incorporating the results of this activity into your church's Children's Sunday (or Sabbath) worship service. This learning activity takes about an hour to complete.

Beginning the Learning Experience
1. As the children enter the room, lead them to sit around the worktable.
2. Hold up a copy of the worship bulletin and ask, "Who knows what this is?" Encourage discussion by asking questions such as: "What is it for?" "How is it used?" Don't feel like you need to correct any "wrong" answers at this point.

3. Ask them if they know who writes the worship bulletin. Explain how the staff and church members try to design a meaningful worship experience for the people on Sunday mornings.

Exploring
4. Ask a child to look up *worship* in the dictionary you provided. Lead the children to brainstorm to come up with a simple definition or description of worship. Write it on the board or flip chart. (You will use this definition later.) The children's definitions may be descriptive (e.g., "When people come to church together to pray and sing to God"). One simple definition is "Confessing that God is God and we are God's people."
5. Ask, "Can someone name the 'parts' of the worship service?" As the children name these, list them on the board or flip chart. (Don't worry if they don't name all aspects of the service.) Some "parts" are:

Objects	Activities	People
the room itself	Bible reading	pastor
hymnal	prayer	the choir
offering plates	children's time	acolyte
instruments	sermon	organist/pianist
altar	liturgical readings	congregation
candles	benediction	worship leader
cross	offering	lay leader
banners	music/singing	ushers

6. Tell the children that you want their help in designing a worship bulletin to help the adults and visitors worship God. Hand out samples of the worship bulletin and hymnals. Have children identify the parts of the worship service they recognize. Identify for them other parts of the corporate worship experience and how they fit into the service.
7. Have the children identify the divisions of the worship service. Explain that some

will be used in the actual bulletin on Children's Sunday. Hand out Children's Sunday Text worksheet and the felt-tipped pens. Have the children copy the divisions and parts of the service. (Remind the children to stay within the spaces of the boxes in their writing.)

8. When they have finished, collect Children's Sunday Text worksheet. Then hand out the Children's Sunday Picture worksheet, the thick markers, and the practice sheet. Explain that they will have a chance to draw the front of the bulletin cover for Sunday. Tell them, "We will try to use each cover drawing," if that is possible in your church. Younger children can work together with older children or with one friend if they want.

Encourage children to think about a good cover for Children's Sunday. Encourage children to use the practice sheet first or to use pencil and then trace their final drawings.

9. Allow enough time for this activity. Walk around, examine the children's drawings, and encourage them as they work. Help those who want assistance.

Concluding the Learning Experience

10. End the session in prayer, thanking God that we can worship in our church and asking God to use the children's work to help others worship.

11. Collect the work that the children have done, and turn it into the church office for production.

Design a Worship Service

CHILDREN'S SUNDAY TEXT

INSTRUCTIONS: In the spaces below, copy the names of the parts (divisions) of the worship service. Try to stay inside the boxes!

Design a Worship Service
CHILDREN'S SUNDAY PICTURE

INSTRUCTIONS: In the box below, draw your picture for the cover of the worship-service bulletin for Children's Sunday.

25. Hymn Writing

It has been said that most of us learn our theology from the hymns we sing. Certainly that is true of children, for whom songs of faith are a formative force in shaping their faith. This activity will encourage children to think about their faith as expressed in favorite hymns and will challenge them to articulate what they believe by writing new lyrics to familiar hymn tunes.

Materials Needed
• Bible
• hymnals
• paper and pencil
• musical instrument for accompaniment (e.g., piano, guitar)
• flip chart or chalkboard

Preparation

If you are not musically proficient, it will be helpful to recruit someone who can play a musical instrument to help the children create their hymn. This activity will be more meaningful to the children if you can incorporate their work in a corporate worship experience. This activity will take about an hour.

Beginning the Learning Experience

1. As the children arrive, hand each one a hymnal. Instruct them to find some of their favorite hymns, if they have any. If they are not familiar with how to use the hymnal, point out the contents and the index of hymn names.
2. As children find favorite hymns, sing one or two verses of each.

Exploring

3. Distribute Bibles and have volunteers look up the following psalms and read them aloud for the group: Psalm 7:17; 13:6; 30:4; 33:1; 59:16; 68:4. Ask them to identify the theme of these passages. ["Sing to the Lord."]
4. Ask one volunteer to read Psalm 33:3, which encourages us to sing a "new" song. Explain that today they will write a "new song" to sing to the Lord by using the tune of a favorite hymn. Encourage the group to decide on a simple tune they can use for this activity (e.g., "Amazing Grace," "Jesus Loves Me," "O Little Town of Bethlehem," "Joyful, Joyful, We Adore Thee," or the hymn tune HYFRYDOL).
5. The next step is a creative process, so there is no one way to go about it. Children may choose a theme for their hymn (praise, thanksgiving), or they can just dive in and call out phrases. Using a chalkboard makes it easier to make adjustments to the lyrics as you go along. As children create their "new song," have them sing it to hear how it sounds.

Concluding the Learning Experience

6. When you and the children are satisfied with the hymn, sing it through one time together. Then encourage the children to give the hymn a name and to copy the text (and the hymn tune name) they've created on their sheets of paper to take with them.
7. Follow up by publishing the text to the hymn in your church newsletter as a handout, or if appropriate, use the children's hymn in a worship service.

26. Symbols in My Church

Children are naturally attuned to symbols, and they absorb much of their faith in their uncritical appreciation for them. This learning activity will help children identify, name, and understand how symbols are used in their church.

Materials Needed
- Bibles
- Signs and Symbols handout
- three-ring binder
- Symbols in My Church filler pages
- markers, crayons
- three-hole punch

Preparation
For this creative learning activity, children will tour the church campus and the sanctuary in search of the faith symbols in their church. You can prepare ahead of time by putting out as many symbols as you can for the children to identify: banners, communion set, candles, pulpit Bible, stoles, robes, etc. Prepare for the class by placing copies of the Signs and Symbols handout on the children's worktable. Prepare the three-ring notebook by creating a colorful cover with the title: "Symbols in My Church" by the children of (fill in name of your church).

Beginning the Learning Experience
1. As the children arrive, greet them by name, and direct them to work on the Signs and Symbols handout on the table. If they want, they can work in pairs with a friend.
2. Give the children a few moments to work on identifying as many signs and symbols as they can; then review their answers by helping them identify any they have missed.
3. Ask the children to name other signs and symbols with which they are familiar. Explain that signs and symbols are important in many ways. Lead them to explore how symbols are helpful by having them tell you how symbols are used, how they are helpful, and what it would be like if we didn't have any symbols.

Exploring
4. Ask the children, "Do you think we use signs and symbols in our church?" Encourage them to name some. Explain the difference between a sign and a symbol. A sign merely names or points to something (e.g., a street sign names a road). A symbol represents something else entirely (e.g., a dove represents the Holy Spirit). Explain that today you want to concentrate on the symbols of your church.
5. Announce that you will all go on a "symbol hunt" through the church. Instruct the children that as you lead them, they are to point out the symbols that they see. Continue to contrast signs and symbols if the children point out signs (e.g., an exit sign or a directional sign).

Make the sanctuary the highlight of your trip. Allow the children to find as many symbols as they can in the worship room, including the layout of the room itself, the baptismal font, Bibles and hymnals, symbols on stained-glass windows, and so forth.

Concluding the Learning Experience
6. Return to the classroom and distribute the Symbols in My Church filler pages, markers, and crayons. Tell the children that they will create a symbols notebook of their church to help others learn about the symbols of their faith. Encourage the children to illustrate as many symbols as they can remember from their "symbol hunt" and to write a brief description of the meaning of the symbols in the space provided. As the children complete the symbols filler pages, have them punch holes along the left margin of the sheets and place them in the three-ring binder.
7. When the children have completed the notebook, place it in an appropriate place for display, such as the church foyer or a welcome center.

Signs and Symbols

1.

2.

3.

4.

5.

6.

7.

8.

9.

10.

11.

12.

13.

14.

Symbols in My Church

What this symbol means: _____

27. Fall Leaf Wax Relief

"GOD IS CREATOR"

Fall is a wonderful time to appreciate God's creation. This Bible learning activity will help children to focus on the creative, natural beauty of God's world and to confess God as Creator.

Materials Needed
- Bibles
- construction paper (one piece, approximately 5" x 6", for each child)
- candles and matches
- yarn
- hole punch
- markers
- glitter spray (nontoxic, nonaerosol)
- newspapers for table covering
- chalkboard

Preparation
This is a fall activity, so be sure there are plenty of leaves on the ground for the children to gather. Cut colored construction paper into pieces approximately 5" x 6", one for each child. You may punch a centered hole near the top of each piece (holding the paper vertically) or allow the children to punch it

themselves. Place newspapers on table to protect the surface.

Because this lesson involves fire and hot wax, be sure that you have adequate adult supervision to assist and oversee the children in the activity. Do not allow small children to handle the matches or lit candles.

Beginning the Learning Experience
1. Welcome the children as they arrive and begin by memorizing Psalm 24:1 (NIV): "The earth is the LORD's and everything in it, the world, and all who live in it." You might play a fill-in-the-blank activity such as the TV game show "Wheel of Fortune." On the chalkboard, draw a blank for each letter in the word or phrase, grouping the blanks for the letters of each word together; do not include the Bible reference. Then have the children take turns guessing a letter. Allow children to guess words they recognize, and continue playing until they have solved the puzzle.

Exploring
2. Take the children outside to look at the fall leaves, and lead them in a discussion about God's creative power. Talk about how nature can teach us about the character of God. Ask them what they learn about God when they look at the sky, the land, trees, animals, and so forth.
3. Invite the children to gather colorful leaves for their next activity. Each leaf should be colorful, small enough to fit within a 5" x 6" surface, and not so dry and brittle that it crumbles when handled.
4. When you return to the classroom, distribute the pre-cut 5" x 6" pieces of construction paper. If you have not already done so, allow the children to punch a hole on their sheets near the top (holding

the paper vertically). Before proceeding to the next step, children are to write a message near the bottom of their sheets that communicates God's creative activity. Ask the children to think of some things they can write, such as "Psalm 24:1," "God made the world," "God is Creator," or "God's handiwork."

5. Establish some safety rules in the use of the candles: roll up long sleeves; pull back loose hair; sit up straight in your chair; do not hold flame close to the leaf or surface of the table. (Do not hesitate to take a lit candle away from a child who refuses to follow safety directions. With young children, have adult volunteers available to handle the candles and melt the wax.)

Demonstrate how to make the wax leaf relief: light the candle and allow one or two drops to fall on the center of the worksheet, and then place the leaf over the wax. This will secure the leaf to the paper. Then the child will continue to drip melted wax from the candle onto the leaf. Dripping a good amount of wax where the edge of the leaf meets the paper will ensure that the leaf stays securely on the paper. Allow the children to melt as much of the candles as they can onto their leaves and paper without danger of burning their fingers on the flames.

Concluding the Learning Experience

6. Collect the candles as children finish melting them, and encourage the children to blow on the melted wax until it cools. Distribute pieces of yarn to loop through the holes punched on the papers, and instruct the children to tie knots or bows for hanging. Spray a little of the gold glitter on the waxed leaf for added decoration (optional).

7. Conclude your lesson by having the children display their fall leaf wax reliefs and by reciting from memory Psalm 24:1, which they learned earlier.

28. Upper Room Communion

Children are intrigued by the observation of Communion (the Lord's Supper) in their church. Often, the ritual seems mysterious; at times, the children may feel left out of this "adult" component of worship. The purpose of this interactive learning activity is to help the children experience what it may have been like to share a Communion meal in the early church.

Materials Needed

- Bibles
- clay oil lamps (optional)
- candles (optional but recommended)
- area carpet (if available)
- large throw pillows
- various wooden bowls
- dipping sauces: yogurt, marinara sauce, applesauce, honey, peanut butter, etc.
- food: bread sticks or pita bread (for dipping), grapes, raisins, nuts, etc.
- cassette, compact disk player, tape or CD with Eastern music (Hebrew or Israeli)
- parchment paper, yellow, off-white, or light brown in color
- two dowel rods
- towels and wipes
- fabric, scarves, towels, or shawls to use as headdresses or shawls
- song sheets (optional)
- adult volunteer

Preparation

Set up the room as an "upper room" would have been in the times of the early church: area rugs on the floor, throw pillows in a circle around the center of the room. For an eating surface, you can use a conference table in the center of the room by laying it "flat" on the floor; in other words, don't raise the table legs. The children may recline or sit on the pillows around the table. Set bowls of food on the table along with the pita bread. These will be used for dipping. Quietly play Eastern music in the background. Prepare the Scripture reading by writing the Bible passage on a large sheet of parchment paper; tape the ends of the sheet to dowel rods to make a scroll.

OPTIONAL: To create more "atmosphere," place oil lamps (use smokeless lamp oil) or candles around the room and use them instead of electric lighting. This activity requires more elaborate set-up, but the learning experience itself should take about an hour.

Beginning the Learning Experience

1. Have one adult dressed in Middle Eastern costume act as host of the dinner, welcoming the children to his or her "home" as they arrive. As the children enter the room, have them remove their shoes as is the Eastern custom, and have someone else available to wipe the feet of the children with a towel or damp cloth. Give each child a scarf or towel to use as a costume headdress or shawl. Then the host may invite the "guests" to relax on the pillows around the table.

2. Announce to the children that they will share a meal similar to one Jesus shared with his disciples and like a meal the first Christians may have shared with one another.

Exploring

3. Lead the children to explore their setting by asking questions about the room, such as, "What do you notice about the room?" and so forth. Explain the custom of Jesus' day of eating by lying on the floor on pillows and rugs and using bread to dip from the food plates. Ask the children to point out the many ways this custom is different from the way they eat at home today.

4. Say: "In the days of the early church, in the Middle East, Jesus' disciples would gather for worship and fellowship and Communion in a setting like this. There were no 'church buildings,' so people would meet in one another's homes. Tonight we meet in the home of

(name of host), a Christian and disciple of Jesus." Invite the children to pretend with you that you are all believers during the days of the early church—just a few years after Jesus died, was resurrected, and ascended into heaven.

5. Have the host explain the procedure for sharing the Communion meal by guiding them through the following order:

a. Use baby wipes or towels to wash the children's hands before the meal. Explain the "foot washing" ceremony with which they were greeted upon arriving today (a social custom of the day but also a lesson by which Jesus showed us how to be servants).

b. Have a prayer thanking God for the meal, the host's hospitality, and the presence of the Spirit of God.

c. Invite the guests to eat the meal by taking a pita or bread stick and dipping it in one of the bowls with peanut butter, marinara sauce, yogurt, honey, and so forth. They can eat the other "finger foods" directly from the bowls.

6. As the children eat, start things off by sharing a favorite story about Jesus—a parable or one of the accounts from the Gospels. Go around the table and ask each child by name, "What is your favorite story about Jesus?"

7. When each child has shared a favorite story about Jesus, announce that you will now have the Scripture reading. Ask for a volunteer and have him or her read from the Scripture parchment. Explain that the "Bible" for the early church was the Old Testament and, later, some of the letters and Gospels.

8. Explain how this meal was similar to the way Jesus ate with his many disciples and friends, such as Mary, Martha, and Lazarus. Dramatically, ask the children to imagine what it might have been like for the disciples to share

that Last Supper with Jesus. Say something like, "You know, Jesus' Last Supper with his disciples was in a room like this. And they reclined on the floor around a table, just like we are. It was dark because it was night, and candlelight was the only light they had. Can you imagine what that must have felt like? Do you remember when someone wiped your feet as you arrived? Does it remind you of a story about the Last Supper?" [Allow the children to respond about Jesus washing the disciple's feet. Explain as necessary.]

9. Ask: "Can you imagine the disciples around the table? Peter may have been sitting there (point to a child), and Andrew over there, and where do you think Judas may have sat? And how about John, 'the disciple that Jesus loved?'" "Do you think they were happy sitting around the table?" "How about when Jesus started to tell them that he had to die? How do you think they felt?" Talk about how hard it must have been for the disciples to think about Jesus leaving them, how Jesus rose from the grave a few days later and saw them again, and how happy the disciples were to be able to have a meal with Jesus again! [Note: Don't rush this part. Allow children time to answer, and keep the discussion conversational as long as the children can stay on track. Encourage questions.]

Concluding the Learning Experience

10. Say, "The last thing the disciples in the early church did before they left the dinner table was to sing a hymn." Let the children suggest a hymn or favorite song. Invite the children to demonstrate the spirit of "servanthood" that Jesus taught them by helping to clean up—it's what a servant would do!

SECTION SEVEN

HOME AND FAMILY

29. Best Memory

Families are the source of many of our best memories. This Bible learning experience will help children remember and share their best memories of self, church, and family.

Materials Needed
- Bibles
- 8½" x 14" cardboard
- self-stick vinyl contact paper (various colors and patterns)
- 8½" x 14" blank paper
- markers, crayons, pencils
- stickers (optional)
- glue or glue guns
- Polaroid camera (optional)
- nine objects for memory game

Preparation
Make a sample memory book to familiarize yourself with the best way to help your children put one together. Gather nine objects and place them on a central display table where the children can view them. This learning activity will take about an hour.

Beginning the Learning Experience
1. Begin this learning experience by inviting the children to examine carefully the nine objects you've placed on a display table (a ball, a book, a pen, a doll, a wood block, and so forth). Tell the children to look at the objects carefully to prepare for an activity.

2. When the children are ready (give them five minutes or so), ask for a volunteer to participate in seeing how good we are at remembering things. Ask the volunteer to turn around and close his or her eyes. Instruct one or two other children to remove two articles from the table. When the volunteer turns around, encourage him or her to guess correctly which articles are missing. Continue this activity, making it more challenging by removing three and then four objects at a time. (You can also set a time limit for guessing which items are missing.)

Exploring
3. Distribute Bibles and invite the children to explore these Bible verses that mention remembering: Genesis 9:12-16; Exodus 20:8; Deuteronomy 8:2; 1 Chronicles 16:12; Psalm 77:11. Ask the children to interpret what is being remembered in each verse and why it is important. (The children may work in pairs and report back to the larger group.)

4. Invite the children to think about some of the best memories they have about their families, church, school, friends, and God. Share some of your own memories with the children to facilitate the conversation. Spend as much time as you can on this step, allowing the children to get excited about sharing their best memories.

5. Show the children the memory book sample you've made. Tell them that they will make a memory book to record some of the memories they have shared.

6. Distribute the materials and instruct children how to make a memory book. Cover the 8½" x 14" cardboard with the decorative contact paper, being careful to smooth out any air bubbles. (You may want to score the cardboard in the center to make it easy to fold later.) Paste an 8½" x 14" sheet of paper to the inside. Fold the cardboard in half, and then fold four sheets of paper and glue one inside the other with a drop of glue along the fold line (see diagram).

Concluding the Learning Experience
7. When the children have completed their memory books, encourage them to begin filling the pages with "best memories." They may describe the memories in writing, illustrate them by hand, use stickers (optional) to decorate their pages, collect

autographs from friends, paste photographs or magazine cutouts, and write some of the Bible verses they have studied. OPTIONAL: You can photograph the children individually using a Polaroid camera, and have them paste the developed photos inside the front covers of their books. Encourage the children to also write their favorite Bible verse or a prayer of thanks to God for remembering us in Jesus.

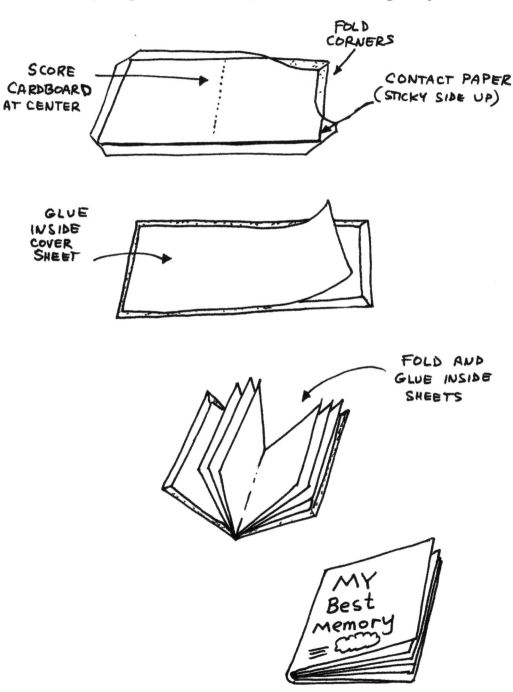

SCORE CARDBOARD AT CENTER

FOLD CORNERS

CONTACT PAPER (STICKY SIDE UP)

GLUE INSIDE COVER SHEET

FOLD AND GLUE INSIDE SHEETS

MY Best memory

30. How to Be Old

Often, groups of people are "invisible" to each other. Many children may not have significant contact with older family members or with the senior members of their church community. Through talking, discussion, and role play, this learning experience will help children appreciate senior citizens in their church and world.

Materials Needed
- Bibles
- old pair of glasses with lenses smeared with petroleum jelly
- cotton balls or ear plugs
- wig
- cane or walker
- string
- gardening or work gloves
- tape
- plastic glass with drinking water (optional)
- spoon and small bowl with cereal (optional)
- What I Learned about How to Be Old handout
- pencils, markers, crayons

Preparation
This can be a wonderful intergenerational learning experience if you allow some of your church's seniors to participate. You may want to seek permission from the parents of the children who will volunteer for the dress-up activity. Make copies of the What I Learned about How to Be Old handout, and have enough markers and crayons for participants. This learning activity will take about forty-five minutes.

Beginning the Learning Experience
1. As the children enter the room, welcome them by name and have them sit in a circle.
2. When the children are focused on you, ask, "How old are you?" or go around the circle and try to guess their ages. Then ask: "How old do you think you'll live to be?" "Who is the oldest person you know?"
3. The American Indians had an expression: "Don't judge a person until you've walked a mile in his moccasins." Ask the children, "What do you think that means?" Say, "Today we're going to learn how to be old. We will learn what God says about older people so that we can appreciate and understand older people better."

Exploring
4. Distribute Bibles to children and have them read some of the following passages that deal with the elderly: 1 Kings 12:8; 2 Chronicles 10:8; Psalm 71:9, 18; Proverbs 20:29; 22:6; Isaiah 46:4; 65:20; 1 Peter 5:5. Ask: "From what you've read, how do you think God wants us to treat older persons?"
5. Choose one or two volunteers to learn to be old. (If you have enough props, all the children can participate.) Ask the children about how they think an old person sees, hears, walks, talks, eats, holds things, and so forth. For each of these areas, allow children to share their perceptions; then explain the reasons why some elderly persons have difficulties in these areas.
6. As you cover each of the areas mentioned (seeing, walking, hearing, and so forth), one at a time, dress the volunteer with the appropriate prop and talk about the change it represents in older people.
SEEING: Have the volunteer put on the smeared glasses and try to read the fine print in a newspaper or in the Bible. Explain that aging causes changes in vision, particularly in an older person's ability to see things close up.
HEARING: Gently stuff cotton or ear plugs in the child's ears, and talk about how getting older often causes hearing loss.
HOLDING THINGS: Put gardening

gloves or work gloves on the volunteer and have him or her try to pick up loose coins or small objects. Have the child try to drink a cup of water or eat out of a bowl while you gently shake his or her elbow. Talk about the effects of arthritis and other diseases that affect senior adults' muscle control and nervous systems.

WALKING: With caution, tie the volunteer's feet with a length of string that causes the child to shuffle when walking. Give the child a cane or a walker to help him or her walk. You might also loop a necktie or scarf around the back of the child's neck and tie the ends to the front of the child's belt to cause a stoop while walking. Explain that aging can cause a weakening of muscles and bones, making it harder for many older people to walk and move as freely as they could when they were younger.

HAIR: Have the child put on a gray wig, and explain how aging causes a change in hair color and texture. Point out that many older people, both men and women, suffer hair loss as well.

7. OPTIONAL: Have the "old volunteers" and a couple of children role-play a common situation between children and elderly (e.g., children in checkout line being impatient with an the elderly person trying to find money to pay for purchase). Remember to debrief after the role play.

Concluding the Learning Experience
8. Help the children reflect on the learning experience by asking questions like the following: "How did it feel to not be able to see, hear, walk, or handle things easily?" "How do you think it would feel to be like this all the time?" "How do you think older people feel when we laugh at them or are impatient with them?"

9. Guide children to apply what they have learned by asking, "What are some things we can do to help older persons?" Distribute the What I Learned about How to Be Old handout and give the children some time to write down or draw what they have learned.

10. Encourage the children to share some of their responses. End the session in prayer.

What I Learned about How to Be Old

_____

_____

_____

_____

_____

_____

_____

_____

_____

_____

_____

_____

_____

_____

_____

_____

_____

_____

_____

_____

_____

_____

_____

_____

_____

_____

_____

_____

_____

_____

31. If Jesus Came to My House

Being Christian means being aware of the presence of God in our lives. This learning experience will help children think about and express ways they can prepare spiritually to practice the presence of God in their lives. At the end of this lesson, children will identify ways they can prepare spiritually for a "visit from Jesus" (the presence of God in their lives).

Materials Needed
- Bibles
- chalkboard
- poster paper
- markers, crayons
- drawing materials
- paper and pencil

Preparation
This lesson offers activity options for children. Set up work areas with materials for each option in different parts of the room. You may want to use your own ideas for activities appropriate for your group. This learning experience takes about an hour to complete.

Beginning the Learning Experience
1. Gather the children in a circle and settle them down by waiting for them to focus on you. When everyone is paying attention, ask, "Have you ever had 'special' or 'important' company come to your house?" Allow the children to share their stories of the special people who have visited in their homes.

Say, "Sometimes, I have special company come to my house, too. Do you know what I do when special company is coming? I get the house ready. Did you do that too when your special guest came?" Ask the children to share some of the special things they had to do to get ready for company. List their responses on the chalkboard.

Exploring
2. Say, "I want to tell you a story of someone who had special company come to his house just as you did. You may know the story already." Read the story about Zacchaeus (Luke 19:1-10) from a children's Bible or from a Bible storybook.

OPTIONAL: If you have a good reader among the children, have one of them read it, or, if you have the story of Zacchaeus on a children's video, show the story in addition to reading it.

3. Ask exploratory questions, such as, "Who was the special company who came to Zacchaeus's house?" [Jesus.] "How do you think Zacchaeus felt when he learned that Jesus was coming to his house?" [Excited, nervous, etc.] "How do you think you would feel if Jesus announced that he would come to your house?" "How would your parents feel if you told them that?"

4. Say: "As in the story of Zacchaeus, Jesus always wants to come to your house. He comes in Spirit, so we can't always see him, but we can feel him. How do you feel when you know that Jesus is with you?" [Let children share their feelings: "safe," "warm," "loved," "happy."]

5. Tell the children to think about Jesus coming to their house. Ask how they can make their house a welcoming place for Jesus. Ask, "What are some ways we make our special company or visitors feel welcome?" [Allow children to answer with suggestions: clean their room, set a place at the table, get a gift, prepare a meal, and so forth.] Refer to the story of how Zacchaeus prepared for his special visitor.

6. Write on the chalkboard, "If Jesus Came to My House…." To help children express ways to make their homes welcoming places for Jesus, suggest that they do one of the following activities or think of one of their own. For the rest of the time together, they will be working on one of these "If Jesus Came to My House" projects.

Options for projects
GROUP ACTIVITIES
- Create and act out a skit of the story of Zacchaeus's preparation.
- Create and act out a skit of what might happen if Jesus came to your house.

INDIVIDUAL OR PARTNER ACTIVITIES
- Write a list of all the things you would have to do to get your house ready for Jesus' visit (physically and spiritually).

- Draw a map to your house so your friends can find their way to visit with you and Jesus.
- Write a short story about what would happen if Jesus came to your house. Include your parents, pets, and friends in your story. What would they say? What would you say? What would you do?

Concluding the Learning Experience
7. Be sure to leave enough time for the children to share their work with the group at large. End the session with prayer, thanking Jesus for visiting our homes and being ever-present in our lives.

32. Mezuzah: God in My House

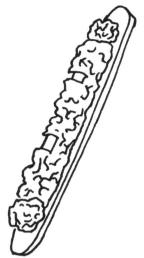

The mezuzah (or mitzvah) is a symbol of the sanctity (or holiness) of the home—in other words, that the home is a holy place where God dwells with us and where we should pray and worship. This learning activity will introduce children to this ancient Jewish custom and give them a way of thinking about how God protects and provides for them in their homes.

Materials Needed
- Bibles
- heavy-duty aluminum foil
- Mezuzah: God in My House handout
- small slips of parchment paper
- fine-tipped markers
- scissors
- glue gun
- 3" x 5" cards
- craft sticks
- nontoxic wood stain
- paper towels

Preparation
For each child, cut the heavy-duty aluminum into 3" x 6" pieces. Cut parchment paper into 2½" x 2½" squares. Prepare a mezuzah sample ahead of time and attach it to the doorpost of the room. On 3" x 5" cards, write the letters, one to a card, to spell out *mezuzah*.

Beginning the Learning Experience
1. Welcome the children as they enter the room. When they are settled and focused on you, ask if they noticed anything different when they walked into the room. Point out the mezuzah that you've attached to the doorpost. Ask if anyone knows what that is. Place on the center of the table the 3" x 5" cards on which you have written the letters that spell *mezuzah*. Challenge the children to unscramble the word.

Exploring
2. Explain that people have many customs about entering a home. Some people wipe their feet on a mat. In some cultures today you take your shoes off before entering the house. In Jesus' time people would wash the feet of the guests. Say that today the class will learn about an old Jewish custom that helps us remember God when we enter a home or a room.

3. Explain the use of the mezuzah, that it is symbolic of the sanctity of the home—reminding us that God lives with us in our homes and protects us. It reminds us that the home is to be a place of prayer and worship, just like church. In Jewish homes the mezuzah is placed on the front door, on the right side as you enter the house, and in every doorway leading into a room in the house. Demonstrate the custom of touching the mezuzah with your right hand as you enter the room and kissing the hand that touches it. The mezuzah is touched again at night when you say your prayers before going to bed.

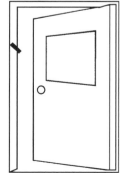

4. Distribute Bibles and explain that each mezuzah contains a little scroll with two handwritten Bible verses. Have the children look up and read aloud Deuteronomy 6:4-9 and 11:13-21. On the reverse side of the small scroll is written one of the names of God, *Shad-dai*, an acrostic for the Hebrew words spelling "Guardian of the houses of Israel."

5. Distribute the materials for making the mezuzah. Have children apply a bit of wood stain on the craft stick and set it aside to dry. Instruct the children to copy Deuteronomy 6:4-9 from their Bibles onto the parchment paper. (They will have to write small, and younger children will need assistance.) Remind them to write, "Shad-dai" on the reverse side of the parchment paper. When finished, they should roll the parchment into a tight scroll.

Next, they must fold the aluminum paper in half and wrap it around the parchment scroll.

OPTIONAL: For a decorative look, wrinkle the aluminum paper and unfold it again before wrapping the parchment.

Have the children punch a small window on the front of the aluminum foil wrapper so that they can just see the scroll. Next, crimp flat the top and bottom of the foil to seal the scroll inside. Glue the sealed scroll to the craft stick using the glue gun.

To finish their mezuzahs, have the children roll up two small balls of aluminum to place at both ends of the rolled and sealed parchments and glue them in place.

Concluding the Learning Experience

6. Distribute the Mezuzah: God in My House handout and review with the students the instructions for how to use a mezuzah in their homes. Encourage the children to explain to their parents the meaning and use of the mezuzah and to ask them for help in placing it in an appropriate place in their homes.

Mezuzah: God in My House

"And write them on the doorposts of your house and on your gates."
—Deuteronomy 6:9

The mezuzah is symbolic of the sanctity (or holiness) of the home because God lives with us there and protects us. It reminds us that the home is to be a place of prayer and worship, just like church. In Jewish homes the mezuzah is placed on the front door, on the right side as you enter the house, and in every doorway leading into a room in the house—except for bathrooms.

The Jewish custom is to touch the mezuzah with your right hand as you enter and leave a room and then kiss the hand that has touched it. The mezuzah is touched again at night when saying your prayers before going to bed.

The mezuzah contains two Bible verses that record God's commandment about remembering God's word: the Shema (Deuteronomy 6:4-9) and the Vehaya (Deuteronomy 11:13-21). On the reverse side of the parchment is the divine name of God, Shad-dai. This is also an acrostic for the Hebrew words that mean "Guardian of the houses of Israel."

Before hanging the mezuzah, it is customary to recite this prayer: "Blessed art thou, Lord our God, king of the universe who has sanctified us with his commandments and commanded us to affix a mezuzah."

The mezuzah is customarily affixed in a slanted position with the upper part pointing toward the inside of the room, on the right doorpost as one enters, in the upper third of the doorpost's height. Using the mezuzah in your home will remind you of God's love and protection and can be an aid to prayer.

33. Needs-Wants Simulation

Children learn early in church that God provides for our needs. This interactive learning experience will help children learn to distinguish the difference between wanting something and needing something.

Materials Needed
- Bibles
- four large paper bags
- plate of liver (optional)
- old catalogues and magazines
- scissors
- glue (optional)
- poster board (optional)

Preparation
On two of the paper bags, in large letters, write the word Need; on the other two write Want. Look through the magazines and catalogues you will use to make sure they are appropriate to use with the children. This learning activity takes about forty-five minutes.

Beginning the Learning Experience
1. As the children arrive, welcome them and have them choose seats around the table. Wait until they are focused on you to begin.
2. Hold up the two large paper bags (or shopping bags) you have already labeled with the words Need and Want. Ask a child to read the words out loud.
3. Say, "I was at the mall the other day, and I saw a mom and dad with their children. As I went by, I saw one of the children point to something and cry, 'Mom, I want that!' The mother said, 'No, we can't get that now.' The child cried louder, 'Why not? I want that!' And the dad said, 'You can't have it; you don't need that.'"
4. Ask, "What word did the child use in asking for the item that caught his attention?" (Hold up the bag with the word Want on it.) Ask: "What word did the father use?" (Hold up the bag with the word Need on it.)

Exploring
5. Distribute the Bibles and have the children read Matthew 6:28-32. Guide the children in exploring and understanding the passage. Say: "Jesus is teaching something about the difference between needs and wants in this passage." Ask: "What example does Jesus give us?" [The lilies (flowers) of the field.] Ask: "How should the lilies be our example in this question of needs and wants?"
6. Write on one side of the chalkboard the word Need and on the other side Want. Ask the children to explain the difference between a need and a want. [A need is something you must have to stay alive, be safe, or to function. A want is something you feel you must have though it is not necessary to live, be safe, or function.]
7. Give an example. Say: "Let's say you come home from school and you get a funny feeling in your stomach. As you do your homework, you hear funny noises coming from your stomach. You try to do your homework, but you can't seem

to think or concentrate. Has this ever happened to you? What's going on?" [You're hungry.] "Is hunger a need or a want?" [A need.] "Your body is telling you that you need to eat to stay alive. So you ask your mom or dad for something to eat. What would you say to your parent?" [I need something to eat.] "Your mom or dad says, 'OK. Here is some liver you can eat.'" [Pull out plate of liver or use some other "yukky" food.] "Then your mom or dad asks, 'What do you want to eat?' What would be your reply?"

At this point, lead the children to understand the difference between the need for food and the choices in wanting something particular to eat.

8. Divide the group of children into two groups. Give each group a set of bags marked Need and Want. Hand out catalogues, magazines, and scissors.

Instruct the children to cut out pictures or words from the magazines and catalogues and place them in the bags according to whether they understand the object to be a "want" or a "need."

OPTIONAL: Have the children in each group paste the pictures on two large posters labeled Want and Need so that they can display it.

Concluding the Learning Experience

9. After the children have had some time for this activity, gather the groups and pull out the pictures in the bags (or on the posters). Discuss with the help of the children how and why each item is either a want or a need. Use questions such as the following to help the discussion along:

• Do you have everything you need?
• Think of someone you know who needs something; tell us about it.
• Who provides for your needs?
• Who provides for the things you want?
• Do you think people sometimes want things that are not good for them? Like what?
• Do you think it's hard to know the difference between what we want and what we need? Why do you think that is?
• Does God give us everything we need? Explain.
• Does God give us everything we want? Why or why not?
• Is it wrong to want things?
• Which things would be good to want even if we don't need them?

10. End the learning experience by leading the children in sentence prayers: each child offers a one-sentence prayer thanking God for supplying what he or she needs.

34. Timely Thank-Yous

Expressing appreciation is a learned behavior as well as an emotional response. This learning experience will help children learn to express appreciation for people who are important in their lives.

Materials Needed

- Bibles
- card stock or different-colored 8½" x 11" heavy paper
- colored markers, crayons, or colored pencils
- watercolors and paint brushes (optional)
- decorative stickers (optional)
- envelopes

Preparation

Make one or two thank-you cards as samples for the children to look at. This learning activity takes between forty-five minutes and an hour.

Beginning the Learning Experience

1. Begin this learning experience by asking children to share some of the "manners" they have been taught: saying "excuse me," saying "please," holding the door open for people, and saying "thank you."

2. Explore with the children why they think we are taught to say "thank you." Explain that saying "thank you" is an expression of gratitude. Work with the children to define what gratitude is—is it a feeling or an act? Or is it both?

Exploring

3. Distribute Bibles and have volunteers read the following verses: Philippians 1:3; Colossians 1:3; Philemon 1:4. Remind them that these Bible books were originally letters written to people. Discuss with the children what these verses express.

4. Lead the children to brainstorm a list of names of persons who are helpful to them around home, church, school, and in activities. Write the names on the chalkboard as children call them out, asking the children to explain in what ways these people help them. Guide the children to think about how these people are gifts from God in their lives.

5. Tell the children that they will have a chance to express gratitude for the people in their lives who help them by creating thank-you cards for them. Distribute materials for making the cards, and allow the children enough time to make cards for those they have named and for any others as they desire. While the children work on their thank-you cards, ask questions about the persons to whom they intend to give the cards and about what those persons have done for them.

Concluding the Learning Experience

6. When children are done creating their cards and addressing the envelopes to the people they want to thank, encourage them to gather the cards before them. Lead the children in a prayer thanking God for the people in our lives who help us and care about us.

SECTION EIGHT

FAITH

35. Birds

One of the ways to faith is to witness God's character and creation. As the psalmist wrote, "The heavens declare the glory of God; the skies proclaim the work of his hands" (Psalm 19:1, NIV). This creative learning activity will help children appreciate and celebrate God's creative imagination.

Materials Needed
- Bibles
- Birds in the Bible worksheet
- watercolors or diluted tempera paint
- small bowls (or large cups) for paint
- smocks or old shirts to use as smocks
- strips of cloth (1" x 12")
- drinking straws
- large art paper or drawing paper
- markers and colored pencils
- paper towels
- illustrations of birds (e.g., photos, posters, drawings, field guide)
- nature music on audio cassette or compact disk (optional)
- newspapers

Preparation
Make enough photocopies of the worksheet for the class. Protect surface areas with newspaper or other covering. Decorating the walls with photos and pictures of birds will enhance the learning experience and will give children ideas for their project. Playing nature music with sounds of birdsong while the children work will add a rich dimension to the activity. This learning activity will take about an hour.

Beginning the Learning Experience
1. Stand at the door as the children enter; greet them by name, and instruct them one at a time to enter and sit at their seats. Preparing the room ahead of time will help with behavior.

2. Engage the children in dialogue about their experiences with birds. Ask if any of them have had birds for pets. See how many kinds of birds the children can name. Ask the children to try to remember as many stories about birds as they can remember. Provide some visuals of birds for the children; a large-format, illustrated book on birds, colorful posters, or a field guide will be useful.

OPTIONAL: If you know someone who has a pet bird, ask him or her to bring it in and talk with the children about its habits, personality, diet, care, and feeding.

Exploring
3. Ask the children, "Did you know that there are a lot of birds in the Bible? Can you think of any stories in the Bible about birds?" Say, "Before we do an activity that has to do with birds, let's look at some places in the Bible that talk about birds. Some may surprise you!"

4. Distribute Bibles and Birds in the Bible worksheets. Encourage the children to work in pairs or in groups of three to collaborate on the worksheet. Tell them that the Scripture passages will give them some ideas for the next activity they will do. (If you have a field guide to birds, you can encourage the children to find a picture of the birds they have identified in the Bible verses.)

5. Once the children have completed the worksheet as assigned (or as much of the worksheet as a predetermined time allows), distribute to each child a large art paper and a pre-cut strip of cloth (1" x 12"). Put out bowls or large cups of diluted watercolor or tempera paint; when brushed on the paper, the paint should be transparent. Direct the children to paint a free and loose, abstract "bird" design by dipping their cloth in the paint and then "swooshing" or dragging it across the paper. Children may mix two or three colors on their paper.

Once the basic design is done, the children may add details with colored markers, crayons, or colored pencils. Demonstrate how they may use the end of a capped marker to impress or scratch feather designs on their bird. Show them how to brush or splatter paint on the surface of the paper and then use a drinking straw to blow air over the wet paint to create "feathers" and "wings."

6. Encourage the children to use their imaginations. Remind them that this is an abstract painting and that God made so many different kinds of birds that anything they paint and draw will be pleasing.

Concluding the Learning Experience

7. While the paintings are drying, have the children cut out frames for their projects from large pieces of construction paper. The inside of each frame should be slightly smaller than the outer edge of the painting. Place the frame over the dried painting and tape from behind.

8. Display the paintings when they are finished. Lead the children to pray in thanksgiving for God's delightful creation of birds.

Birds in the Bible

Directions: Look up the following passages in the Bible
and identify the birds mentioned.

Genesis 1:20-22 _____

Genesis 8:6-12 _____

Genesis 15:9 _____

Deuteronomy 14:12-18 _____

1 Kings 17:6 _____

Job 39:13 _____

Job 39:26-27 _____

Psalm 84:3 _____

Psalm 104:17 _____

Psalm 105:40 _____

Proverbs 26:2 _____

Song of Solomon 2:12 _____

Isaiah 16:2 _____

Isaiah 40:31 _____

Isaiah 46:11 _____

Jeremiah 8:7 _____

Jeremiah 12:9 _____

Jeremiah 17:11 _____

Ezekiel 39:4 _____

Matthew 10:29 _____

Matthew 23:37 _____

Mark 4:4 _____

Luke 3:22 _____

Luke 12:24 _____

36. Faith Shields

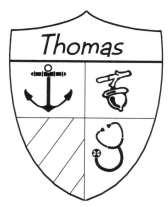

This learning experience will help children think about their faith and how it relates to their concept of God, personality, and aspirations.

Materials Needed
- Bibles
- Faith Shield template
- scissors
- markers, crayons, pencils
- construction paper
- glue or glue sticks
- rulers or straight edges
- book of heraldry or pictures of actual family crests

Preparation
Create a sample Faith Shield of your own to illustrate the concept to the children. Trace and cut out of cardboard or card stock enough copies of the Faith Shield template to share one among two or three children. Younger children may need assistance with the layout of their shields. This learning activity will take about an hour.

Beginning the Learning Experience
1. Welcome the children as they enter the room. When they are focused on you and you are ready to begin, ask if any of them can describe what a shield is. Allow the children to give you any number of descriptions; then tell them that you want to talk about a specific kind of shield.

2. Explain to the children that shields are both for protection and identification. Tell them that in medieval days, when knights wore a lot of armor and helmets that covered their faces, the designs on their shields helped identify who they were. That way you could tell if someone else was a friend or foe. Show examples of shields and crests from a book of heraldry or a similar resource.

Exploring
3. Tell the children that today they will make a faith shield. A faith shield helps you tell others some important things about yourself. Show your sample faith shield and explain the five panels they will use: top horizontal bar—their name; left upper—a symbol representing their idea of God; right upper—symbols of their faith; left lower—three stripes of their favorite color; right lower—a symbol of what they hope to be or do in their lives (see illustration).

4. Prompt the children to help you think of appropriate symbols for some of the panels: GOD: rock (steadfastness, dependable, never changing); mountain (awesome, big); bird or bird's wing (Holy Spirit or protector); anchor (grounding); Bible, cross, cloud (mystery) FAITH: tree (growing); praying hands (seeking); flower (open, receiving); egg (young and forming); ship (seeking).

5. Distribute Faith Shield templates and materials. Instruct children to use the template to trace a shield on their poster board and then to cut out the shield. Direct them to draw their symbols on construction paper and to cut out the shapes. Ask probing questions about the symbols they choose.

Concluding the Learning Experience
6. When the children are finished, have them display and share their faith shields with the other children in the class.

Faith Shield

37. Fish

Learning how to see everyday things and events from a spiritual perspective helps us understand that everything in our lives is imprinted by the hand of God. This creative learning experience will help children appreciate God's creative power in a common but favorite creature.

Materials Needed
- Bibles
- drawing paper or construction paper
- chalk pastels
- white glue in squeeze bottles
- large construction paper (for optional frame)
- wipes or moist paper towels
- spray fixative
- hair blow-dryer (optional)
- pictures or photographs of fish
- nature recording of ocean waves
- masking tape or stapler (optional)

Preparation
Cover surface areas to protect them from chalk dust. You may want to keep damp paper towels handy for a quick cleanup as the children work on their projects. Because of the fumes, remember to use the spray fixative only in a space with adequate ventilation—outdoors, if at all possible. This learning activity will take about an hour to complete.

Beginning the Learning Experience
1. Welcome the children as they enter the room, and direct them to their seats. Set a quiet mood for the lesson by playing "mood music" of ocean waves.
2. Ask the children to close their eyes and to listen to the sound of the waves on the beach. Use guided imagery to lead the children to picture themselves on the beach. Describe feelings and sensations they experience: the warmth of the sun, the heat and

grit of the sand, the breeze on their skin, the salty smell of the ocean, the sand between their toes, and so forth.

Next guide them to imagine swimming in the ocean and seeing all the fish under the water. Describe some of the colorful fish they can see. As children keep their eyes closed, ask them to describe other fish they see. Ask prompting questions, such as, "Do you think fish see things with their eyes, just like we do? Do fish get cold? How do fish sleep? How fast can fish swim? Do fish play? How?" After a few minutes, bring the children back slowly from this guided imagery experience.

Exploring
3. Tell the children that one of the things we learn about God from nature is that God has a wonderful imagination. God seems to love variety! We can see this in the incredible variety of fish God has made. Show some pictures of fish from books, posters, slides, magazines, and so forth. Be sure to include some pictures that show underwater plants and point out the variety God has created there as well. Encourage the children to share what they imagine the underwater environment looks like.
4. Ask the children to share some stories of fish they've encountered—pet fish, fish they have caught when fishing, fish they have eaten, and so on.

5. Ask, "Can you think of stories in the Bible that talk about fish?" Allow the children to relate some stories they remember. Have the children look up some of these "fish stories" in the Bible: Job 41:7; Ecclesiastes 9:12; Isaiah 19:8; Ezekiel 47:9-10; Jonah 1:17; Matthew 17:27; Luke 5:4-7; 24:42; John 21:9-13.

6. Distribute art paper and chalk pastels. Demonstrate to the children different ways to draw fish. Remind them that fish come in all colors, shapes, and designs—there is no wrong way to draw a fish! Encourage the children to draw at least three fish—or a whole school of them—using the pastels. Instruct them to paint the surrounding water and background and to include plants. Show them how to use two or three colors for each fish and to blend them with their fingers. (Provide wipes or damp paper towels to clean their hands.)

7. As the children work, ask exploratory questions: "What do you think God was thinking when God made so many different kinds of fish?" "Tell me about your fish."

"Why did you choose that color?" "Are you glad that God made so many colors?"

8. When they are done drawing their fish and have completed the background, have them outline the fish (scales, eyes, fins, and so forth) and plants and other underwater objects with white glue from the squeeze bottles. When the glue dries, it will leave a raised outline on the drawing.

Concluding the Learning Experience

9. When the children are finished with their pictures, spray the paper with fixative to secure the chalk. Let the glue dry before the children take their pictures home. (Use a handheld hair dryer to expedite the process, if necessary.)

OPTIONAL: Use large construction paper to create a frame for the children's pictures. The inside of the frame should be smaller than the art paper. Tape or staple the frame to the picture.

10. Conclude this learning experience with prayer, thanking God for the beauty and variety of colors and shapes of fish and all the plants that live underwater.

38. God Is Light

We know God mostly through analogies. The Bible speaks of God variously as being like a rock, a shepherd, a hen, a king, and a devouring fire, among other things. The Bible uses the metaphor of light to talk about God's Word and God's character, and as a way of understanding how believers reflect God's love. This lesson will help children begin to appreciate the analogy of God as light.

Materials Needed
- Bibles
- large sheets of butcher paper or drawing paper
- beeswax sheets for candles and wicks
- modeling clay (to form a base) or unfinished wooden candleholders (one for each child)
- newspaper to cover table surfaces
- markers, crayons, or finger paint
- self-stick mailing labels
- newspapers

Preparation
Beeswax sheets can be found in most craft stores, or if you know of other ways of making candles, consider using them for this activity. Use caution when using hot wax around children. Protect work surface with newspapers. This learning activity will take about an hour.

Beginning the Learning Experience
1. As the children enter, welcome them and have them sit around the table.
2. Tell them that you want them to guess the topic for today's lesson by playing Hangman, a game in which the children take turns guessing the letters in a secret word that is represented on the chalkboard by a certain number of blanks—in this case, five blanks representing the letters in the word *light*. Each incorrect letter

guess is penalized by adding a piece of the gallows or a body part of a hanged stick figure. (See chapter 14 for more complete directions on how to play.) Continue the game until someone guesses the word. You may have one child volunteer to draw the picture.
3. Tell the children, "We are going to talk about a special kind of light today." Divide the class into two or three teams, depending on the number of children, but having no more than four children on a team if possible. Give them about two minutes to brainstorm as many different kinds or sources of light as they can. Allow the children to use markers, crayons, or finger paint to list the kinds of light and draw pictures of them on a large sheet of butcher paper or a large sheet of drawing paper.
4. When you call time, have a volunteer collect the markers and/or paint. Then review the drawings. The team that has illustrated the most kinds of light wins.
5. Ask questions about light: "Was it hard to draw light?" "What light do we have in this room right now?" "Is there light that we cannot see?" "Do you know how fast light travels?" "Have you noticed that when there is lightning, we see the light before we hear the thunder? Why is that?"

6. Tell the children to be silent and to close their eyes. Tell them you want them to imagine they are entering the front doors of their houses. Tell them to go through their houses in their minds and count the number of lights they have at home. After a few moments go, around the room and ask each child to tell you the number of lights he or she counted. Write the number on a self-stick label and have the child stick it to his or her shirt. Tell the children that when they get home, they should count again to see how well they remembered.

Exploring

7. Distribute Bibles. Tell the children that they will read about another source of light. Read, or have children read, these passages:

Genesis 1:3	God created light.
Psalm 119:105	The Bible is a light for us.
Proverbs 4:18	The path of just people is like light.
Ecclesiastes 11:7	God's light is sweet.
Matthew 5:14	Jesus says we are the light of the world.
Luke 8:16	Do not hide your light.
John 9:5	Jesus says, "I am the light of the world."

8. After exploring with the children what each passage means, tell them that they will make something to remind them about what the Bible says about light.

9. Distribute the beeswax, wicks, and candleholders or clay, and give instructions to the children about how to make a roll-up beeswax candle. Demonstrate how to lay the beeswax sheet flat on the table and place the wick about one-quarter inch inside one edge, making sure that at least one-half inch of the wick hangs over one edge. To shape the candles, simply roll the beeswax sheet around the wick. When the candles are finished, children will put them in the candleholders you provided, or they can make candleholders out of clay. (Allow them to use their imagination in creating their clay candleholders.)

10. On a decorative label or card, have the children write the words, "Jesus said, 'I am the light of the world,'" to keep next to their candle.

Concluding the Learning Experience

11. Conclude this learning experience by having the children help with the room cleanup. Then gather to pray together to thank God for creating light and for sending Jesus to be the light of the world.

39. Spiritual Genograms

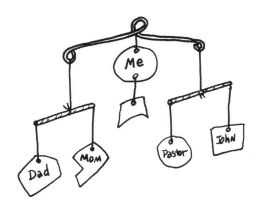

We all grow in the spiritual life to the extent that others help us grow in faith. A genogram is a graphic representation of family relationships. This learning activity, which is an adaptation of the use of genograms to show spiritual relationships, familial and otherwise, will help children identify those people in their lives who have helped them grow in faith.

Materials Needed
- Bibles
- 11" x 17" paper or large construction paper
- scissors
- pencils, markers, or crayons
- string or yarn
- drinking straws
- construction paper
- hole punch
- flash cards with compound words (half a word to a card)
- fun foam sheets (different colors)
- felt-tip markers (permanent ink)
- shapes templates (optional)
- Spiritual Genograms handout

Preparation
Make a sample Spiritual Genogram. Make copies of the Spiritual Genogram handout for the children to take home, and have enough materials on hand for every child. Younger children may need a little more guidance with this activity, but they can appreciate how others help them in their faith. This activity takes about an hour to complete.

Beginning the Learning Experience
1. Welcome the children as they enter the room, and direct them to be seated around the table.
2. Ask, "Who can tell me what a compound word is?" Show flash cards of sample compound words, and ask children to identify the two words that make up the compound word displayed (e.g., sidewalk, boardwalk, breakfast, grandmother, and so forth).
3. Show the card with the word *genogram* on it. Ask if they can figure out what that compound word means (geno = meaning "kind"; gram = meaning "written or drawn"). Let them guess, and then explain that the word is used for a drawing of those of our kind, our family.
4. Show a sample genogram of your own family or of a biblical family (e.g., Adam and Eve and their children; Abraham and Sarah and their children). Explain the structure of the genogram and its conventions: (a) circles represent females and squares represent males; (b) persons are represented in birth order from left to right; and (c) deceased persons are indicated by an X inside the symbol. Encourage the children to make a genogram of their own family.

Exploring
5. Tell the children that today they are going to make "spiritual genograms." Spiritual genograms represent those people, places, or things that have helped our faith. Show an example of your own spiritual genogram.
6. In order to help the children create their genograms, suggest that they answer

questions, such as: "Who first taught me about God?" "Who first taught me how to pray?" "Who taught me about faith?" "Who taught me how to behave?" "What people do I admire because of how they live the Christian life?" "Where do I feel closest to God?" "Where do I feel it is easiest to worship?" "Who do I admire in my family who is very religious?" "Who in church teaches me about God?"

7. Distribute materials for the craft. Ask the children to write the names of their spiritual mentors and ancestors in the faith (the people who have been teachers and role models to them) on the fun foam. (Use felt-tip permanent markers.) The children can cut out shapes around the names to represent their relationships to those individuals, or just cut out simple shapes, such as squares, circles, and triangles. Direct the children to put the names in some kind of order (e.g., chronological, by family relationship, by "closeness" association).

8. Direct the children to put their spiritual genograms together in the form of a mobile. Distribute straws, scissors, and yarn or string. If you have a sample genogram mobile, show it to the children. As the children work on their mobile genograms, ask exploratory questions about the relationships of the persons and places on their genograms. Help them make connections among the components of their genogram. (Don't let them forget to include themselves in the genogram!)

Concluding the Learning Experience

9. If you have time, let the children explain their spiritual genograms. Have them explain the components and the connections. Ask leading and clarifying questions: "How are these people connected to you?" "How many are family members?" "Which of these people are friends?" "What have you learned about God from these people?" "How many of these people know each other as well as you?" Have the children help you with the cleanup.

Spiritual Genograms

A spiritual genogram is a way to show how others influence and shape your spiritual life. Many people have taught you about faith—for instance, your parents, grandparents, people at church, pastors, teachers, and friends. To help you create your own spiritual genogram, answer the following questions:

Who taught you to pray?

_____

Who taught you to be kind?

_____

Who first taught you about God?

_____

Who in church teaches you about Jesus?

_____

From whom in church do you learn most about what God is like?

_____

Who taught you how to read the Bible?

_____

Who taught you how to read a hymnal?

_____

Who makes you feel special?

_____

Who helps you feel happy and glad?

_____

Now, make a mobile to show the people in your spiritual genogram. Use different shapes and colors. Write the names of the persons in your genogram in the shapes, and tell what they taught you about faith, God, Jesus, and so forth. Hang your spiritual genogram mobile in a visible place that will remind you of the people in your life who love you and care about you.

40. Make a Joyful Noise

Praising God is a spontaneous and natural expression in the Christian life. This learning experience will encourage children to express joy in praising God, as the Bible tells us to do.

Materials Needed
- Bibles
- empty small canisters or coffee cans
- string and yarn
- muslin fabric or chamois cloth
- wooden dowels and bamboo rods
- baby food jars
- popcorn kernels, dried beans, and/or uncooked rice
- buttons
- wire
- aluminum pie plates
- metal juice can covers
- plastic or metal funnels
- tape
- sandpaper
- wooden blocks
- just about anything that will bang, rattle, twang, ring, or chime!
- audio cassette or compact disk player (optional)

Preparation
Gather materials for making musical instruments. You may want to make some samples ahead of time to model for the children. Allow them to have the freedom to be creative in making their own instruments, however. Anything that makes a sound can be an instrument! You may of course provide ready-made musical instruments: tambourines, kazoos, guitars, flutes, harmonicas, and so forth.

Beginning the Learning Experience
1. Begin this learning experience by asking the children to think of sounds that express emotions. Call the children up one at a time to make a sound, and have the rest of the group try to guess what emotion is associated with the sound (e.g., sobbing = sadness; growl = anger; chuckle = pleasure; laugh = happiness; grunt = displeasure; gasp = surprise, etc.).

Exploring
2. Tell the children that you want to explore one emotion that is mentioned in the Bible. Distribute Bibles and have children look up

and read 1 Chronicles 15:16, where David told the leaders of the priests to appoint singers to sing joyful songs, accompanied by musical instruments. Then read Psalm 100:2, where we are instructed to worship the Lord with gladness and with joyful songs. Ask the children to name things they can be joyful about. Memorize Psalm 100:2 together.

3. Allow the children to gather materials to make their musical instruments. Suggest ways they might construct them, but encourage them to use their imaginations in creating their instruments.

Rhythm drums can be made of muslin fabric or chamois cloth, string or yarn, and empty, round canisters. (Coffee cans work well.) Stretch the fabric or cloth over one opening, secure with string, and decorate as desired.

Chimes can be made by hanging metal or bamboo rods from string. Use a small wooden dowel to strike out a rhythm.

Shakers and rattlers can be made by filling small baby-food jars with dry beans, unpopped popcorn kernels, or rice. Secure the lid and shake! Buttons strung on string or wire make great sistrums, an ancient rhythmic instrument.

Cymbals can be improvised from aluminum pie plates. Attach the plates to string or punch holes to attach grips. Metal juice can covers and fruit juice drink tops make good finger cymbals.

Horns can be made from pieces of (clean) garden hose and plastic or metal funnels. Just tape the hose to the funnel and blow!

Rhythm sticks are as simple as two dowels used to strike out a rhythm. Wrap sandpaper around each dowel and rub together for a different sound.

Concluding the Learning Experience

4. Conclude this learning experience by working with the children to create joyful noise. Practice a rhythm, play a song on the cassette or CD player and play along, or just loudly recite Psalm 100:2 to a rhythm. Vary the ways to make a joyful sound: play the instruments slowly, then faster; play soft, then loud, then soft again; stand in a circle and begin a rhythm and have the person next to you pick it up, followed by the next one, and so forth.

Recommended Resources

Bellecci–St. Romain, Lisa. *Building Family Faith Through Lent: Lectionary-Based Activities.* Liguori Publications, 1997.

Bolton, Barbara. *How to Do Bible Learning Activities: Grades 1-6.* Ventura, Calif.: International Center for Learning, 1982.

Cronin, Gaynell Bordes. *The Best of Holy Days and Holidays: Prayer Celebrations with Children.* Minneapolis: St. Anthony Messenger Press, 1997.

Fiarotta, Phyllis, and Noel Fiarotta. *The You and Me Heritage Tree: Children's Crafts from 21 American Traditions.* New York: Workman Publishing Co., 1976.

Fulbright, Pat H. *Termites on the Ark: Creative Ideas for Teaching Children.* Macon, Ga.: Smyth and Helwys Publishing, 1998.

Griggs, Patricia. *Creative Activities in Church Education.* Nashville: Abingdon Press, 1980.

_____. Using Storytelling in Christian Education. Nashville: Abingdon Press, 1982.

Heiberg, Jeanne. *Advent Arts and Christmas Crafts: With Prayers and Rituals for Family, School, and Church.* Paulist Press, 1995.

_____. *Arts and Crafts for Lent: From Mardi Gras to Passiontide, with Prayers and Blessings for Family, School, and Church.* Paulist Press, 1997.

Hickerson, Neva. *Bible Times Crafts for Kids.* Ventura, Calif.: Gospel Light, 1993.

Huffman, Margaret Anne. *Advent: Worship & Activities for Families.* Nashville: Abingdon Press, 1998.

James, Darcy. *Easter Is Jesus: Lenten Devotions and Activities for Families.* Nashville: Abingdon Press, 1992.

Keilly, Sheila, and Sheila Geraghty. *Advent & Lent Activities for Children: Camels, Carols, Crosses, and Crowns.* Twenty Third Publications, 1996.

Lynn, David. *Quick and Easy Activities for 4th–6th Graders.* Grand Rapids: Zondervan Publishing House, 1991.

O'Gorman, Thomas. *Advent Sourcebook.* Liturgy Training Publications, 1990.

O'Neal, Debbie Trafton. *Before and After Christmas: Activities for Advent and Epiphany.* Minneapolis: Augsburg Fortress Publications, 1991.

_____. *Before and After Easter: Activities and Ideas for Lent to Pentecost.* Minneapolis: Augsburg Fortress Publications, 1993.

Polek, David, and Rita Anderhub. *Advent Begins at Home.* Liguori Publications, 1980.

Price, Cheryl. *Bible Learning Centers.* Carthage, Ill.: Shining Star Publications, 1989.

Revoir, Trudie West. *Legends and Traditions of Christmas: Devotional Ideas for Family and Group Use During Advent.* Revised by John H. Pipe. Valley Forge, Pa.: Judson Press, 1998.

Runk, Wesley. *Jesus, the Light of Our Lives: Nine Children's Object Lessons for Lent and Coloring Book.* C.S.S. Publishing. Co., 1993.

Scorer, Donna. *52 Crafts for the Christian Year.* Kelowna, B.C.: Wood Lake Books, 1998.

Stroup, Laverne Kelvington. The Creative Factor. St. Louis: Christian Board of Publication, 1990.

Sullivan, Kim. *Beach Party Crafts for Kids.* Ventura, Calif.: Gospel Light, 1998.

_____. *Safari Crafts for Kids: Includes Projects for Children from Preschool to Sixth Grade.* Ventura, Calif.: Gospel Light, 1996.

Williamson, Nancy S. *52 Ways to Teach Memory Verses.* San Diego: Rainbow Books, 1998.

_____. *52 Ways to Teach Stewardship.* San Diego: Rainbow Books, 1998.